STATE ARCHIVES OF ASSYRIA

VOLUME II

State Archives of Assyria Cuneiform Texts (SAACT) is a series of text editions presenting central pieces of Mesopotamian literature both in cuneiform and in transliteration, with complete glossaries, name indexes and sign lists generated electronically from the transliterations. The goal of the series is to eventually make the entire library of Assurbanipal available in this format.

Set in Times
Typography and layout by Teemu Lipasti
Typesetting by Greta van Buylaere and Mikko Luukko
The Assyrian Royal Seal emblem drawn by Dominique Collon from original
Seventh Century B.C. impressions (BM 84672 and 84677) in the British Museum
Cover: Etana ascending to heaven on eagle's back (VA 8795)
Courtesy Vorderasiatisches Museum, Berlin

Printed in Finland
by Vammalan Kirjapaino Oy

ISBN 951-45-9047-3 (Volume 2)
ISSN 1455-2345 (Series)

STATE ARCHIVES OF ASSYRIA CUNEIFORM TEXTS

VOLUME II

The Standard Babylonian

Etana Epic

CUNEIFORM TEXT, TRANSLITERATION, SCORE,
GLOSSARY, INDICES AND SIGN LIST

By
Jamie R. Novotny

with the assistance of
Simo Parpola

THE NEO-ASSYRIAN TEXT CORPUS PROJECT
2001

ACKNOWLEDGMENTS

The present volume has grown out of an idealistic attempt to compile and present the central works of Standard Babylonian myths and epics, in both the cuneiform text and in transliteration, not only for the purpose of teaching, but also to make the primary source material more readily available to whoever wishes to consult it. Although this goal is far from complete, this volume, as well as SAACT 1, has brought this dream one step closer to reality.

I would like to thank Simo Parpola, the director of the Neo-Assyrian Text Corpus Project, for his assistance with the arrangement of the post-Tablet II material and the nature of the various concurrent editions of the Epic, editing the volume, and for restoring some badly damaged passages; his suggestions and restorations have contributed a great deal to the finished product. Also, I would like to express my thanks to A. Barron, who has pointed out errors, typos, and inconsistencies as well as provided valuable, practical aid in the production of the final manuscript, as well as A.K. Grayson, the director of the RIM Project, and J. Jones, the undergraduate administrator of the Department of Near and Middle Eastern Civilizations, for reading through the introduction of this volume, offering criticisms and improvements.

I am grateful to Dr. Beate Salje, Director of the Vorderasiatisches Museum (Berlin), for granting permission to publish the photograph of VA 8795 used on the cover of this volume.

Furthermore, this volume has benefited from the scholarly work of M. Haul. His careful study, edition, copies, and collations of the Neo-Assyrian recension of Etana have been utilized here. It would certainly be an injustice not to acknowledge the work of this Assyriologist, especially since I was unable to personally collate the tablets as originally planned.

I would like to thank Dr. L. Shiff, as well as the Social Sciences and Humanities Research Council of Canada who support the Royal Inscriptions of Mesopotamia Project, whose archives were an invaluable resource in the preparation of this volume.

I am grateful to A.K. Grayson, R.F.G. Sweet, and G. Frame for all the time and care that they have taken in order to properly train me in Akkadian and Sumerian language and literature; Dr. R.M. Talbert of Virginia Commonwealth University for introducing me to the fascinating world of Mesopotamia; H. Grau, the RIM Project administrator, and M. da Mota, the graduate administrator of the Department of Near and Middle Eastern Civilizations, for their continued support in various ways; and, last but by no means least, my parents, Bob and Diana, and my sister, Jennifer, for their ongoing support and encouragement.

Toronto, January 2001 Jamie R. Novotny

CONTENTS

INTRODUCTION

The Etana Epic, known in antiquity (after its incipit) as "They Planned out a City" or the "Series of Etana," narrates the story of an eagle, a serpent, and Etana, a king of Kiš. This literary composition is known from Old Babylonian (Larsa[?] and Susa), Middle Assyrian (Assur), and Neo-Assyrian (Nineveh) recensions. Even though the earliest exemplars of the epic date to the early second millennium, the story of Etana's flight into the heavens was certainly known by the last half of the third millennium, since this heroic ascent is recorded in The Sumerian King List and a man mounted on an eagle, probably Etana, is depicted on Old Akkadian cylinder seals. The Neo-Assyrian, or Standard-Babylonian version, comprising fourteen exemplars, is the most complete recension, but portions of the composition, including the conclusion, are still missing. Due to the fragmentary condition of the epic, many uncertainties about the composition remain, the two most problematic being the length of the narrative, and the arrangement of the post-Tablet II material (see below).

All the Neo-Assyrian sources, with the exception of exemplars B_2 and B_3, are presently housed in the collections of the British Museum, London. Exemplar B_3 ("Pittsfield fragment") is now in the Berkshire Museum in Pittsfield, Pennsylvania, and exemplar B_2 ("Marsh fragment") is presently in the Bryn Mawr College Library, Pennsylvania. The fourteen Neo-Assyrian exemplars, all from the Library of Assurbanipal in the North and SW Palaces of Nineveh, belong to several different copies or editions of the Etana series; there were at least three to four editions, ranging from single-column to three-column tablets (see Haul Etana, p. 164 and n. 494). For example, the scribe of the single-column exemplar B_3 designates the narrative of the serpent and the eagle as "Tablet II" (DUB 2.KÁM), while the scribe of the double-column exemplar A (K 2606) places it in "Tablet III" (DUB 3.KÁM) of the series.

Aim and Content of the Volume

The present volume presents a reconstruction of the Standard Babylonian recension of the Etana Epic, based on all available exemplars, and hopes to be a useful tool for teaching purposes. It is, however, far from being regarded as a full-scale critical edition, as the computer-generated text produced from the transliteration is in essence a modern transcription, not a copy, and no translation or textual commentary has been incorporated. The present manuscript, on the other hand, does contain a brief introduction to Etana, a selected bibliography, a list of manuscripts, a computer-generated text in Neo-Assyrian script, an up-to-date transliteration with variant apparatus, a score of the manuscripts used, a sign list, a key to the logograms, and complete computer-generated glossaries and indices in the SAA style. Since the arrangement of the material differs from the editions of J.V. Kinnier Wilson (*The Legend of Etana,* Warminster 1985), C. Saporetti (*Etana*, Palermo 1990), and M. Haul (*Das Etana-Epos*, Göttingen 2000) as well as the translations of S. Dalley (*Myths from Mesopotamia* [Oxford 1989], pp. 189-202) and B.R. Foster (*Before the Muses* 1 [Bethesda 1993], pp. 449-460), three concordances have been provided for comparative purposes. Since the line count differs from the earlier editions, it is recommended that the present volume be cited as **SAA Etana**.

Although there are gaps in Tablets I and III of the Standard Babylonian recension, the earlier Old Babylonian and Middle Assyrian versions generally have not been integrated into the reconstruction of the composition, as this would have confused the historical relation between the three editions. It has already been pointed out by J.S. Cooper (JAOS 97 [1977], pp. 508-512) that there does not appear to have been a straight line of transmission from the OB recension to the MA one, and from the MA edition to the NA one. In addition, the episodes preserved in all three recensions often present their own account of the story, which makes it very difficult, if not impossible, to harmonize the narrative of the SB recension with that of the MA and OB versions. Primarily for these two reasons, the earlier versions of the Epic have not been fully used in the present reconstruction. Lines in them closely paralleling the SB version have, however, been included in the score and variant apparatus, and also used for restorations.

Editions and Translations of the SB Version

The Neo-Assyrian recension of the Etana Epic was mentioned for the first time in Assyriological literature in 1876 by George Smith in his *The Chaldean Account of Genesis* (London 1876), pp. 138-144. It has been edited, in part or in full, by E.T. Harper (BA 2 [1894], pp. 391-408), P. Jensen (KB 6/1 [1900], pp. 100-115 and 581-588), P. Dhorme (*Choix des textes religieux assyro-babyloniens* [Paris 1907], pp. 162-181), S. Langdon (*Babyloniaca* 12 [1931], pp. 1-53), J. Siegelová (*Kritické zpracoavání mytu o Etanovi* [Prague 1967]), J.V. Kinnier Wilson (*The Legend of Etana* [Warminster 1985], pp. 81-139), C. Saporetti (*Etana* [Palermo 1990], pp. 46-117), W. Horowitz (*Mesopotamian Cosmic Geography* [Winona Lake 1998], pp. 50-57), and recently by M. Haul (*Das Etana-Epos*, [Göttingen 2000], pp. 163-230). The editions by Kinnier Wilson, Saporetti and Haul not only offer hand copies of the original cuneiform tablets, and transliterations and translations of the tablets that have been identified as part of the Neo-Assyrian version, but also provide complete and up-to-date studies of Etana, reconstructions of the plot, as well as useful bibliographies. Hand copies, transliterations and translations of the OB and MA versions are also an integral part of Kinnier Wilson's, Saporetti's and Haul's editions of Etana.

The SB version of the Epic has been translated, in part or in full, by G.A. Smith (*The Chaldean Account of Genesis* [London 1876], pp. 138-144), A. Ungnad (*Die Religion der Babylonier und Assyrer* [Jena 1921], pp. 132-139), E. Ebeling (in ATAT[2] [1926], pp. 235-240), R.J. Williams (*Phœnix* 10 [1956], pp. 70-77), E.A. Speiser and A.K. Grayson (in ANET[3] [1969], pp. 115-118 and 517), R. Labat (*Les religions du Proche-Orient asiatique* [Paris 1970], pp. 294-305), K. Lyczkowska (*Przeglad Orientalistyczny* [Warsaw 1972], pp. 31-34), S. Dalley (*Myths* [1989], pp. 189-202), and by B.R. Foster (*Before the Muses* 1, Bethesda 1993, pp. 449-460, and *From Distant Days* [Bethesda 1995], pp. 102-114). The translations of Dalley and Foster can be used as companions to this volume. One should, however, be advised that the arrangement of the post-Tablet II material and the line count differ from the present volume. For a comparison of Dalley's and Foster's arrangement of the Epic, see below and Concordance of Tablet and Episode Numbers II.

Bibliographies of the Etana Epic and related matters can be found in Kinnier Wilson Etana, pp. 17-19, Saporetti Etana, pp. 145-150, Haul Etana, pp. 231-246, and in G.J. Selz, *Acta Sumerologica* 20 (1998), pp. 171-179.

Summary of the Story

Tablet I opens with the great gods designing and building the city Kiš for mankind. After its completion, the city needed a human representative worthy of supervising its teeming population. Enlil and Ištar painstakingly searched through all the cult centres in the land for a suitable candidate and, as a result, Etana was duly nominated. Thus, kingship, and all the responsibilities associated with it, descended from its sublime place in the heavens to the earth for the first time. Unfortunately, at this point, there is a break of about twenty-six lines. The text briefly resumes with a fragmentary passage (interpretation uncertain) in which Etana's wife relates a dream to her husband. After ten lines, the narrative breaks off, this time until the end of the tablet.

Tablet II begins with a poplar tree growing in the shade of some structures, including a cultic platform dedicated to the god Adad, presumably erected by Etana. Here, a serpent builds its nest in the roots, while an eagle constructs its abode in the crown of the tree. After an unspecified time, the two neighbours mutually swear an oath of friendship in the presence of the divine judge Šamaš, the sun-god, and offer to take care of each other's young by sharing the responsibility of feeding them. For a while, both respect the pact and take turns hunting a cornucopia of wild beasts: boars, bisons, gazelles, mountain goats, and other creatures of the steppe. One day, after his young have grown up, the eagle maliciously plots to devour the serpent's offspring. Despite the persistent efforts of the youngest bird in the nest to dissuade his father from performing this unprovoked act of aggression, the bird of prey swoops down from the crown of the poplar, destroys the serpent's nest, and devours all of his companion's offspring.

Upon returning from a hunting expedition, the serpent discovers that all of his children are missing. After conducting a careful investigation, it suspects foul play on the part of the eagle, as incriminating evidence is left behind. The serpent immediately implores Šamaš to avenge his loss. The divine judge, who witnessed the horrific deed, accepts his pleas, strikes down a wild ox and advises the serpent to hide in the innermost organs of the carcass and wait. When his adversary comes to feed on the flesh, he is to seize him, pluck out his feathers, clip his wings, and cast him into a deep pit to die from starvation and dehydration. Heeding the advice of the sun-god, the serpent sets out on his journey into the mountainous terrain, discovers his hiding place, and sets up camp. A little while later, the ravenous bird of prey, in search of his next meal, spots the carcass of the ox, and begins to circle above it with his young. The youngest of the nest, suspecting that Šamaš has managed to transform the body of the deceased animal into an ingenious trap, warns his father. Ignoring the warnings of his offspring, the eagle swoops down from the sky and begins to inspect the wild ox. As suggested by the sun-god, the serpent springs forth from his hiding spot, seizes the bird of prey, plucks out his feathers, clips his wings, and casts his former friend into a deep pit. The eagle, left for dead, pleads to the divine judge, but aid is refused. Eventually moved by the continuous pleas, Šamaš sends a human agent to help him, since he could not perform the rescue himself as a result of the eagle's violation of the friendship oath.

Meanwhile, back in Kiš, Etana had been imploring the sun-god daily to grant him an heir, as the conventional methods of obtaining divine assistance — offerings of lamb's blood, incense, and fattened sheep — failed to attract the attention of Šamaš. Finally, Šamaš gives in and appears to the desperate king, presumably in a dream. The divine judge informs Etana about the plight of the invalid eagle and advises him to save this bird only if he promises to assist him in finding the mythical herb facilitating fertility, the so-called "plant of birth." Etana immediately embarks on his quest and, very soon after departing Kiš, he discovers the pit housing the crippled eagle.

Tablet III opens with Etana standing at the edge of the pit as the eagle discusses with Šamaš his means of communicating with mankind. The Kišite king, overly excited by being able to communicate with an eagle, forgets to introduce himself to the starving and dehydrated bird and forcefully demands that the eagle hand over the highly-prized "plant of birth." Immediately after Etana rescues his new traveling companion, the bird sets out upon the quest for the elusive mystical herb, however in vain, as the "plant of birth" is not to be found anywhere on the surface of the earth. The eagle promptly suggests that they should seek aid from the goddess Ištar. At this suggestion, Etana immediately mounts the gargantuan bird and the two begin their ascent into the "heavens of Anu." At each "double-mile," the eagle asks Etana to describe the features of the land and sea. After attaining a lofty altitude of three leagues, the Kišite king looks down, panics, loses his courage, and begs the eagle to take him back to Kiš. The two rapidly descend to the comforts of solid ground.

At this point, the narrative breaks off for about thirteen lines. When the text resumes, it appears that Etana and his winged companion have returned to Kiš. The narrative for the next twenty lines is fragmentary and seems to deal with the retelling of one or two favourable prognostic dream(s). The extremely damaged condition of the fragments makes it impossible to determine the precise significance of the episodes and who was the recipient(s) of the vision(s) of the night. The first dream may deal with the location of the "plant of birth," while the second(?) deals with a flight into the heavens (interpretation uncertain).

After a break of approximately eight lines, the narrative resumes with Etana informing the eagle of a bizarre dream that he just had. In the night vision, Etana and his feathered friend pass through the entrance of the Gate of Anu, Enlil, and Ea and that of the Gate of Sîn, Šamaš, Adad, and Ištar. At each of the gates, the two bow down and respectfully pay homage. After passing through the latter gate-structure, the curious Kišite king enters a house where he sees a goddess, probably Ištar, sitting upon her throne. Lions are stationed at its base. As Etana approaches the divine lady, the lions rush towards him, but before being mauled, the Kišite king wakes up, shaking violently. The eagle, upon hearing this, suggests that the dream is a favourable premonition and that they should fly into the heavens once again.

Etana takes his seat on the back of his feathered friend and the two soar three leagues upwards. They arrive safely and pass through the Gate of Anu, Enlil, and Ea and the Gate of Sîn, Šamaš, Adad, and Ištar. At this point, the text breaks off again and, unfortunately, the conclusion of the Epic is completely missing, apart from a few traces of signs. It is hence not known for certain whether or not Ištar provided Etana with the elusive "plant of birth" and if the Kišite king was finally able to sire an heir as a result of this divine intervention. According to one tradition, The Sumerian King List, Etana was succeeded by his son Balih as the king of Kiš.

Length of the Composition

As mentioned above, due to the fragmentary nature of the Epic, many uncertainties about the composition remain. One of the most problematic questions is the length of the narrative. From the extant source material, there is no doubt that the Etana Epic was at least a three-tablet series, but it might have been longer.

S. Langdon (*Babyloniaca* 12 [1931], pp. 2 and 52) proposed that it was originally narrated on four tablets. This hypothesis has been accepted by a number of Assyriologists, including B.R. Foster (1993) and S. Parpola (personal correspondence), and is preferred in the present volume. On the basis of a four-tablet series, with each tablet containing approximately one hundred and fifty lines, the Etana Epic would have been narrated in its Standard Babylonian form in about six hundred lines.

S. Dalley (*Myths* [1989], p. 189), however, suggests that the Etana Epic was a slightly shorter composition in its Standard Babylonian edition, and was a three-tablet series consisting of about four hundred and fifty lines. This proposal is accepted by M. Haul (*Das Etana-Epos* [2000], p. 2).

J.V. Kinnier Wilson (*The Legend of Etana* [1985], pp. 2-3), on the other hand, suggests that the Etana Epic was a relatively long composition and was composed on at least six tablets, but, more probably, it was written on eight. In addition, he proposes that the series had to be completed on an even number of tablets. However, a length of six to eight tablets seems very unlikely, as we currently possess nothing beyond Tablet III (or Tablet IV, according to Langdon). The suggestion that the narrative had to be concluded on an even number of tablets is likewise unjustified, since Enuma Eliš, Erra, Anzû, Nergal and Ereškigal, as well as the Descent of Ištar, were all completed on an odd number of tablets.

The Arrangement of the Post-Tablet II Material

Like the length of the composition, the arrangement of the post-Tablet II material is very problematic. Every scholar who has worked on the Epic seems to have his or her own opinion as to how the episodes relate to one another. Here only the editions of Langdon, Kinnier Wilson, Saporetti, and Haul, the study and partial edition of Etana's ascent into the heavens by Horowitz, as well as the translations of Dalley and Foster will be compared.

Before diving into the discussion of how the various scholars arrange the post-Tablet II material, some preliminary remarks need to be made about some of the exemplars, as their nature ultimately determines how the material is to be arranged.

Exemplar C (82-3-23,6), a text fragment measuring 5.4 x 5.8 cm, contains ten lines on the obverse and eleven on the reverse. Unfortunately, it cannot be securely assigned to Tablet I or III. In addition, 82-3-23,6 has no duplicates and does not physically join any other exemplar. Although it is very possible that exemplar C may belong to Tablet I (thus Kinnier Wilson Etana, pp. 84-87, and Haul Etana, pp. 33 and 96), it has been tentatively assigned to Tablet III, between lines 56 and 100, following a suggestion made by S. Parpola (personal correspondence).

Exemplar H (79-7-8,43), a fragment measuring 4.3 x 3.2 cm, begins with a conversation between the eagle and Etana on the obverse; the reverse ends with Assurbanipal colophon d (Hunger Kolophone no. 319), preceded by a fragmentary catch line ending in]-⌜*ṣa*?⌝-*ar*. The tablet appears to have been a single-column tablet (Assurbanipal edition as indicated by the colophon). The obverse of 79-7-8,43 (lines 1-11) is taken in the present volume as a duplicate of exemplar N (K 3651+), lines 9-19 (= SAA Etana III 9-19). However, earlier editions and translations considered 79-7-8,43 either as a fragment physically joining exemplar N (K 8578 only) or as a fragment containing a passage similar to K 3651 + K 8578, lines 9-19. Compare the editions of Langdon and Kinnier Wilson, as well as the translations of Foster.

Exemplar J (K 14788), a fragment measuring 2.6 x 2.6 cm, contains nine lines on one side. Unfortunately, it cannot be securely assigned to either Tablet I or III. In addition, it is unclear if the passage belongs to the obverse or reverse of the tablet. Like 82-3-23,6 (exemplar C), K 14788 has no duplicates and does not physically join any other exemplar. However, it has been suggested that this fragment may belong to the same edition (Assurbanipal single-column edition) as exemplar M (Haul Etana, pp. 33 and 99).

Exemplar M (K 19530 + Rm 2,454 + 79,7-8,180) is a single-column tablet (Assurbanipal edition) measuring 8.9 x 7.2 cm and large coherent passages are preserved on both faces. One side narrates a failed attempt to reach Ištar's heavenly palace and the subsequent return to Kiš (Side A = SAA Etana III 31-56), while the other deals with a dream of Etana, its interpretation, and a successful flight into the heavens (Side B = SAA Etana III 106-144). Unfortunately, since the episode or episodes linking the two passages together is missing, it has been a serious problem determining which side is the obverse and which is the reverse. It has been suggested that the obverse of a tablet is generally flatter than its reverse (Horowitz, *Mesopotamian Cosmic Geography* [1998], p. 48). If this is the case, then Side A would be the obverse and Side B the reverse. However, the problem is not that simple, since K 19530+ partially duplicates exemplars K (K 8563) and N (K 3651 + K 8578). Luckily, it is known that the latter source is a single-column tablet. This is evident from the fact that both its obverse and reverse overlap passages on both faces of exemplar N (= SAA Etana III 31-38 and 134-144). Unfortunately, it only duplicates K 8563 on one side (= SAA Etana III 106-117). To complicate the situation even further, the nature of exemplar K (K 8563), up until recently, has been a major crux in reconstructing the narrative (see below). Previous editors of Etana have toyed with the idea that K 8563 was either a single- or double-column tablet, but never really considered that it could have had three columns on each side. The determination between the obverse and the reverse of K 19530+ ultimately depends on the nature of K 8563.

Exemplar K (K 8563), a fragment measuring 7 x 5.3 cm, contains a fragmentarily perserved dream of Etana's wife on one side (Face A = SAA Etana I 57-66) and a prognostic vision of the Kišite king, its interpretation, and the beginning of the successful ascent into the heavens on the other (Face B = SAA Etana III 100-117). As mentioned above, Face B is partially duplicated by exemplar M (= SAA Etana III 106-117), while Face A has no known parallels. Furthermore, since the last eight lines on Face A are completely destroyed, it has been a serious problem determining where the dream of Etana's wife is to be placed in the Epic, as its association — or its lack thereof — to the contents of Face B is not immediately evident. Since the episode or episodes linking the two passages together is missing and since the right side of Face A, that is the left of Face B, is completely broken off, it has been a problem not only figuring out which side is the obverse and which is the reverse, but also whether K 8563 was originally a single- or multi-column tablet.

S. Langdon (*Babyloniaca* 12 [1931], pp. 43-44 and 52) and S. Dalley (*Myths* [1989], p. 199) have suggested that exemplar K was a single-column tablet which contained material from the same tablet of the Etana series on both its obverse and reverse. Langdon assigned K 8563 to Tablet IV in his reconstruction and believed that the episode narrated on Face A was on the reverse, while those of Face B were on the obverse. He also assumed that Side B of exemplar M (K 19530+), the face narrating the successful ascent, was the obverse and Side A of the same tablet, the face detailing the failed flight into the heavens and the subsequent return to Kiš, was the reverse. For him, the dream of Etana's wife was the conclusion of Tablet IV and the Epic. On the other hand, Dalley assigned K 8563 to Tablet III, but considered Face A as the obverse and Face B as the reverse. Since the latter partially duplicates Side B of K 19530+, she therefore considered the face narrating the successful ascent as the reverse (Side B) and the side detailing the failed flight as the obverse (Side A). Based on this arrangement, the dream of Etana's wife immediately followed the Kišite king's return to Kiš and preceded Etana's prognostic vision and successful flight.

J.W. Kinnier Wilson (*The Legend of Etana* [1985], pp. 108-111 and 124-125) has suggested that exemplar K was originally a double-column tablet which contained material from two consecutive tablets in the Etana series. According to his reconstruction, he felt that the obverse (columns i and ii) narrated material from Tablet IV and the reverse (columns iii and iv) detailed the contents of Tablet V. Since Face B of K 8563 (column i) partially duplicates Side B of K 19530+ and contains the episode of Etana's prognostic vision and the very beginning of the successful ascent, he considered this side not only to be the obverse of exemplars K and M, but also as the obverse of Tablet IV. Furthermore, since columns ii and iii of K 8563 (now completely destroyed) would have narrated the reverse of Tablet IV (= Side A of exemplar M) and the obverse of Tablet V (column iv) — that is the dream of Etana's wife — would therefore have been narrated on the reverse of Tablet V and would represent the final passage of that tablet in the Etana series.

More recently, M. Haul (*Das Etana-Epos* [2000], pp. 29-32) has suggested that exemplar K was originally a triple-column tablet which contained the entire composition, that is all three tablets in the Etana series. The obverse would have contained all of Tablet I (columns i and ii) and the first half of Tablet II (column iii), while the second half of Tablet II (column iv) and all of Tablet III (columns v and vi) would have been copied on the reverse. Since Face B of K 8563 (column vi) partially duplicates Side B of K 19530+ and contains the episode of Etana's prognostic vision and the very beginning of the successful ascent, he considered this side to be the reverse of exemplars K and M as well as the reverse of Tablet III. Based on this reconstruction, the obverse of K 8563 (column i) therefore has to be part of the obverse of Tablet I. If this proposal proves to be correct, then the following can be said about the arrangement of the post-Tablet II material: 1) Face A of K 8563 — that is the dream of Etana's wife — is to be regarded as the obverse, and is to be considered as part of the obverse of Tablet I (= SAA Etana I 57-66); 2) Face B of K 8563 and Side B of K 19530+ — that is Etana's prognostic vision, its interpretation, and the successful flight into the heavens — are to be regarded as the reverse of both exemplars, and these episodes are considered as being narrated on the reverse of Tablet III (= SAA Etana III 100-144); and, 3) Side A of K 19530+ — that is the failed ascent and subsequent return to Kiš — is to be regarded as the obverse, and is considered as part of the obverse of Tablet III (= SAA Etana III 31-56).

This arrangement of the post-Tablet II material is very plausible, especially in light of a recent study of SAA Etana III 1-8 (exemplar N; only K 8578) which argues that this passage narrates how Šamaš harmonized the speech of the Kišite king and the gargantuan bird of prey (J.R. Novotny, "How Etana and the Eagle were permitted to communicate with one another," forthcoming). This episode, if interpreted correctly, fits perfectly into the natural progression of the narrative only if it is placed at the very beginning of Tablet III, not halfway through it. Since the obverse of K 3651 + K 8578 (exemplar N) duplicates material from the obverse of K 19530+ (exemplar M; Side A = the side with the failed flight and subsequent return to Kiš, and the reverse of exemplar N duplicates material from the reverse of exemplar M (Side B = the side with the successful ascent), then there should be no doubt that the Kišite king and the eagle ascended a distance of three leagues into the "heavens of Anu" not once, but twice, providing that Šamaš granted Etana and the eagle the ability to speak the same language in SAA Etana III 1-8.

Now that the main difficulties concerning the arrangement of the post-Tablet II material have been addressed, the various proposals of S. Langdon, J.W. Kinnier Wilson, S. Dalley, C. Saporetti, B. Foster, W. Horowitz, and M. Haul can be illuminated.

Langdon (*Babyloniaca* 12 [1931], pp. 39-53) suggests that the arrangement of the material is as follows: 1) SAA Etana III 1-19 (exemplars H + N [only K 8578]) represents the beginning of his Tablet III; 2) SAA Etana III 100-144 (exemplars K, M [only Rm 2,454], and N [only K 3651]) represents the obverse of his Tablet IV; 3) SAA Etana III 14-56 (exemplars M [only Rm 2454], N [only K 3651], and O) is considered as the reverse of his Tablet IV; and, 4) SAA Etana I 57-66 is the conclusion of his Tablet IV as well as the composition. In addition, Langdon believes that exemplar J (SAA Etana uncertain placement) belongs to another literary work.

Kinnier Wilson (*The Legend of Etana* [1985], pp. 104-125) arranges the episodes as follows: 1) SAA Etana III 70-91 belongs to his Tablet I; 2) SAA Etana III 1-19 (exemplar H with restorations from exemplar N) represents the beginning of his Tablet III; 3) exemplar J (SAA Etana uncertain placement) is the very beginning of his Tablet IV; 4) SAA Etana III 100-144 (exemplars K, L, and M) is considered as the obverse(?) of his Tablet IV; 5) SAA Etana III 1-56 (exemplars M, N, and O) and SAA Etana III 133-163 (exemplar N) represent the reverse(?) of his Tablet IV; and, 6) SAA Etana I 57-66 is the final passage narrated on his Tablet V. In addition, he places several other fragments into the narrative, but their association with the Etana Epic is uncertain.

Dalley (*Myths* [1989], pp. 196-200) suggests that the post-Tablet II material should be arranged in the following manner: 1) SAA Etana III 1-56 represents the obverse of her Tablet III; 2) exemplar J (SAA Etana uncertain placement) and SAA Etana I 57-66 are placed between SAA Etana III 56 and 100; and 3) SAA Etana III 100-144 is considered the reverse of her Tablet III.

C. Saporetti (*Etana* [1990], pp. 92-117) suggests that the episodes are to be arranged in the following order: 1) SAA Etana I 57-66 immediately follows Tablet II; 2) SAA Etana III 70-80; 3) SAA Etana III 100-144; 4) SAA Etana III 81-91; 5) SAA Etana III 155-163; 6) SAA Etana III 1-56; 7) exemplar J (SAA Etana uncertain placement); and, 8) exemplar H verso, which contains Assurbanipal colophon d. Since he does not divide the story according to its ancient division, but uses his own tripartite system, it is not possible to determine which tablet or tablets he considered the episodes to be narrated on.

B. Foster (*Before the Muses* [1993], pp. 456-459, and *From Distant Days* [1995], pp. 109-114) follows the arrangement of Langdon, but omits SAA Etana I 57-66 and III 70-91. W. Horowitz (*Mesopotamian Cosmic Geography* [1998], pp. 47-57) places SAA Etana III 100-163 before III 1-56; he does not comment on the position of SAA Etana I 57-66 and III 70-91.

The arrangement of the Epic by M. Haul (*Das Etana-Epos* [2000], pp. 7-33 and 166-211) essentially agrees with the present volume. The only exception is that exemplar C is here inserted between III 56 and 100 following a suggestion by S. Parpola, whereas Haul lists this fragment as uncertain placement.

In any event, the problems surrounding the length of the composition, the arrangement of the post-Tablet II material, and exactly how the story ends will continue to be debated until new manuscripts of the Etana Epic are discovered or positively identified.

Cuneiform Text and Sign List

The cuneiform text and sign list have been generated automatically from the composite transliteration using programs and fonts specially created by the Neo-Assyrian Text Corpus Project for the publication of this cuneiform text series. The black characters indicate that the sign is preserved in at least one exemplar, whereas the white characters represent modern restorations and correspond to items within square brackets in the transliteration. For the indication of partially preserved signs, see below. Portions of the text that cannot be restored are indicated by the shaded areas.

The sign list contains all the phonetic and logographic sign values occurring in the composite text as well as their frequencies. The sign numbers displayed in bold are those published in R. Borger, *Assyrisch-babylonische Zeichenliste* with minor modifications.

Transliteration

The reconstruction of the Standard Babylonian Etana Epic presented here is in principle exclusively based on the relevant tablets and fragments discovered at Nineveh (Kuyunjik). Earlier versions of the Epic have, however, been taken into consideration when they closely parallel the SB version. The transliteration is not oriented after any specific exemplar, but is a conglomeration of several different manuscripts. The goal of the volume is to provide a composite text of the Epic, so that it is possible to read it in class without constantly being forced to restore damaged areas, which may occur in the individual manuscripts. The composite text rests on a score transliteration of all the relevant published sources. The score has been included in this volume.

Most exemplars of the SB Etana appear to have been written on either single- or multi-column tablets. Regardless of whether the text was written on the former or latter type, the column divisions of the originals as well as the distinction between obverse and reverse have been ignored. Instead, each line of the composite text has been assigned a running line number taking into account the number of lines lost in the breaks.

In some exemplars, two consecutive lines have been combined together and are marked with a division mark ":" separating the hemistichs. Such lines have been systematically split into two consecutive lines in the text. The division mark ":" however, has been retained in the text and placed at the end of the line preceding the ":" sign, not at the beginning of the line following this divider.

The transliteration system in this volume follows the conventions of the SAA series. One should note that the cuneiform font employed in this volume only distinguishes between completely preserved and broken signs. On account of this, partially preserved signs, those enclosed by half-brackets, appear as "destroyed" in the cuneiform text. Half-brackets enclosing signs whose readings are certain have generally been removed from the composite text; however, they have been retained in the score transliteration.

Variant Apparatus

Although the present volume is not intended to be a critical edition of the SB recension of the Etana Epic, the variant apparatus contains all variants occurring in the Neo-Assyrian version, including merely orthographic variants such as *tú* for *tu*, etc. As a rule, only first-millennium exemplars have been taken into consideration systematically. Variants from the earlier OB and MA versions have however been included where their text closely parallels the SB version.

Glossary and Indices

The list of logograms, glossary and indices have been electronically generated and follow the conventions of the SAA series. The glossary contains all lexically identifiable terms occurring in the text, including restored passages. The variants occurring only in the variant apparatus, following the practice of the SAACT series, are not included in the glossary or other indices.

MANUSCRIPTS

TABLET I

A = K 2606 i. Double-column tablet. Lines 1-30. Copies: Harper, BA 2 (1894) 461 and 463; Langdon Etana, pl. 7; Kinnier Wilson, Iraq 31 (1969), pl. 2; Kinnier Wilson Etana, pl. 11; Saporetti Etana, pl. 1; Haul Etana, pl. 3. Photograph: BA 2 505.

K = K 8563 i. Three-column tablet. Lines 57-66. Copies: Harper, BA 2 (1894) 451; Langdon Etana, pl. 9; Kinnier Wilson Etana, pl. 30; Saporetti Etana, pl. 2; Haul Etana, pl. 9.

Other sources

$\mathbf{OB}_{M}$ = MLC 1363 (Morgan Tablet). A three-column OB tablet of unknown provenance (Larsa?) paralleling or duplicating the contents of Tablet I and II of the SB recension. Column i parallels lines 9-17, 27. Copies: Scheil, RT 23 (1901) 18-21; Clay, YOR 5/3, pl. 3; Clay, BRM 4, pl. 2; Langdon Etana, pl. 12; Kinnier Wilson Etana, pl. 1; Saporetti Etana, pl. 8. Photograph: Clay, YOR 5/3, pl. 7.

$\mathbf{B}_{3}$ = Berkshire Museum 7.6. See Tablet II. The colophon preserves the first line of Tablet I.

For additional information on the tablets, see Haul Etana, pp. 91-102.

TABLET II

A = K 2606 iv. Double-column tablet. Lines 153-155. Colophon line reads: [*x*] LIBIR.RA.BI.GIM *šá-ṭir-ma ba-ri* IM.DUB ^{m}*x x*[...]. Copies: Harper, BA 2 (1894) 463; Langdon, Etana, pl. 7; Saporetti Etana, pl. 1; Haul Etana, pl. 4.

B = K 8572 (+) BMC T-236 (+) Berkshire Museum 7.6. Single-column tablet with Assurbanipal colophon (B_3). Lines 1-59 and 94-155. All three fragments belong to the same tablet but have not been physically joined.

B_1 = K 8572. Lines 1-7. Copies: King, CT 13, pl. 31; Kinnier Wilson Etana, pl. 13; Saporetti Etana, pl. 1.

B_2 = BMC T-236 (Marsh Tablet). Lines 34-59 and 94-122. Copies: Jastrow, BA 3 (1898) 379 and 381; King, *First Steps in Assyrian*, pp. 204-206 and 212-214; Langdon Etana, pls. 1-3; Kinnier Wilson Etana, pls. 14-15 and 17-18; Saporetti Etana, pl. 1. Photograph: BA 3 385.

B_3 = Berkshire Museum 7.6. Lines 7-39 and 121-159. Copies: Jastrow, JAOS 30 (1909-10) 130-131; Langdon Etana, pls. 1 and 3; Kinnier Wilson Etana, pls. 13-14 and 18-19; Saporetti Etana, pl. 1. Photographs: JAOS 30 between 130-131.

F = K 2527 + K 5299. Single-column tablet. Lines 44-119. Copies: Harper, BA 2 (1894) 439 and 441; King, *First Steps in Assyrian*, pp. 206-212; Langdon Etana, pls. 4-5; Ebeling, AfO 14 (1941-1944), pl. 12; Kinnier Wilson Etana, pls. 15-18; Saporetti Etana, pl. 1; Haul Etana, pls. 5-6. Photographs: BA 2 503 and 507.

G = K 1547. Single-column tablet. Lines 81-101 and 129-148. Copies: Harper, BA 2 (1894) 443 and 445; King, *First Steps in Assyrian*, pp. 209-212; Langdon Etana, pls. 5-6; Kinnier Wilson Etana, pls. 16-19; Saporetti Etana, pl. 1; Haul Etana, pls. 7-8. Photographs: BA 2 503 and 507.

Other sources

$\mathbf{OB_M}$ = MLC 1363 (Morgan Tablet). Lines 116-131. See Tablet I.

$\mathbf{OB_S}$ = Susa Tablet. Lines 20-47, 53-72. A single-column OB tablet from Susa (Elam) paralleling or duplicating the contents of Tablet II of the SB recension. Its present location is not known. Copies: Scheil, RA 24 (1927) 106; Langdon Etana, pls. 13-14; Kinnier Wilson Etana, pls. 2-3; Saporetti Etana, pls. 9-10.

$\mathbf{MA_1}$ = A 142. Lines 5, 18-36, 98-112. A four-column MA tablet from Assur paralleling or duplicating the contents of Tablet II and III of the SB recension. Copies: Ebeling, AfO 14 (1941-1944), pls. 9-10; Ebeling and Köcher, LKA, pls. 21-22 no. 14; Kinnier Wilson Etana, pls. 5-6; Saporetti Etana, pls. 4-5.

$\mathbf{MA_4}$ = VAT 10529. Lines 141-148. A single- or double-column MA tablet from Assur paralleling or duplicating the contents of Tablet II of the SB recension. Copies: Ebeling, KAR 1 no. 170, 2; Langdon Etana, pl. 6; Kinnier Wilson Etana, pl. 10; Saporetti Etana, pl. 7. Collations: Haul Etana, pl. 13.

TABLET III

C = 82-3-23,6. Lines 70-92. Copies: Kinnier Wilson, JNES 33 (1974) 238; Kinnier Wilson Etana, pl. 12; Saporetti Etana, pl. 3. Photograph: Kinnier Wilson Etana, pl. 32. Collations: Haul Etana, pls. 13-14.

H = 79-7-8,43. Single-column tablet with Assurbanipal colophon. Lines 9-19 and 159-169. Copies: Harper, BA 2 (1894) 447; Langdon Etana, pl. 8; Kinnier Wilson Etana, pls. 20-21; and, Saporetti Etana, pls. 1 and 3. Photograph: BA 2 507.

K = K 8563 vi. Three-column tablet. Lines 100-117. Copies: Harper, BA 2 (1894) 449; King, *First Steps in Assyrian*, p. 200; Langdon Etana, pl. 9; Kinnier Wilson Etana, pl. 23; Saporetti Etana, pl. 1; Haul Etana, pl. 10. Photograph: Harper, BA 2 (1894) 509.

L = 83-1-18,489. Lines 102-111. Copies: Kinnier Wilson, Iraq 31 (1969), pl. 3; Kinnier Wilson Etana, pl. 22; Saporetti Etana, pl. 1. Collations: Haul Etana, pl. 14.

M = K 19530 + Rm 2,454 + 79-7-8,180. Single-column tablet. Lines 31-56 and 106-144. Copies: Harper, BA 2 (1894) 453, 455, and 457; King, *First Steps in Assyrian*, pp. 200-203; Langdon Etana, pls. 10-11; Kinnier Wilson Etana, pls. 24-25; Saporetti Etana, pl. 1. Photograph: BA 2 505 and 509. Collations: Haul Etana, pl. 14.

N = K 3651 + K 8578. Single-column tablet. Lines 1-38 and 133-143. The reverse of K 8578 is very badly damaged, and it has not been utilized in the reconstruction of the text. Copies: Harper, BA 2 (1894) 447 and 459; Langdon Etana, pls. 8-9; Kinnier Wilson Etana, pls. 26-28; Saporetti Etana, pl. 1; Haul Etana, pls. 11-12. Photographs: BA 2 503 and 507; Kinnier Wilson Etana, pl. 32; Horowitz, Or. 59 (1990) pl. 90.

O = Rm 522. Lines 25-43. Copies: Harper, BA 2 (1894) 459; Langdon Etana, pl. 11; Kinnier Wilson Etana, pl. 23; Saporetti Etana, pl. 1. Photograph: BA 2 509.

Other sources

MA$_2$ = VAT 10291. A MA tablet from Assur paralleling or duplicating the contents of Tablet III of the SB recension. Copies: Ebeling, AfO 14 (1941-1944), pl. 11; Kinnier Wilson Etana, pls. 7-8; Saporetti Etana, pls. 6-7; Haul Etana, pls. 1-2. Photogaph: Kinnier Wilson Etana, pl. 32.

MA$_3$ = VAT 10137. Lines 133-137. A four-column MA tablet from Assur paralleling or duplicating the contents of Tablet III of the SB recension. Copies: Ebeling, AfO 14 (1941-1944), pl. 12; Kinnier Wilson Etana, pl. 9; Saporetti Etana, pl. 5. Collations: Haul Etana, pl. 13.

A = K 2606 iv. See Tablet I. The catch line preserves the first line of Tablet III.

B_3 = Berkshire Museum 7.6. See Tablet II. The catch line preserves line 1 of Tablet III.

UNCERTAIN PLACEMENT

J = K 14788. Lines 1-9. Copies: King, Cat. Suppl., p. 130 no. 1335; King, CT 34, pl. 18; Kinnier Wilson Etana, pl. 22; Saporetti Etana, pl. 2.

Other Tablets and Fragments Attributed to Etana

K 1578 NA fragment. Copy: Kinnier Wilson Etana, pl. 31.

K 9610 NA fragment. Copy: Kinnier Wilson, JNES 33 (1974) 238.

K 10099 NA fragment. Copy: Kinnier Wilson Etana, pl. 21 (= his exemplar I).

K 13859 NA fragment. Copy: Kinnier Wilson Etana, pl. 31.

Rm 398 NA fragment. Copy: Kinnier Wilson, JNES 33 (1974) 238.

Rm 2,492 NA fragment. Copy: Kinnier Wilson, JNES 33 (1974) 245; Etana, pl. 29 (= his exemplar P).

Sm 157 + Sm 1134 NA fragment. Copies: Thompson Gilg., pl. 54; Kinnier Wilson, Iraq 31 (1969), pl. 3.

Sm 1839 NA fragment. Copies: Kinnier Wilson, Iraq 31 (1969), pl. 2; Kinnier Wilson Etana, pl. 11 (= his exemplar B); Saporetti Etana, pl. 1.

81-2-4,391 NA fragment. Copies: Kinnier Wilson, JNES 33 (1974) 245; Kinnier Wilson Etana, pl. 31.

IM 51345 OB fragment. Copies: J.J. van Dijk, TIM 9 no. 49; Kinnier Wilson Etana, pl. 4 (= his exemplar OV_3).

VAT 10566 MA fragment. Copy: Ebeling, KAR 2, no. 332.

VAT 11232 MA fragment. Copy: Ebeling, KAR 2, no. 342.

VAT "11653" MA fragment. Copies: Ebeling, KAR 2, no. 335; Kinnier Wilson Etana, pl. 10 (= his exemplar MA_5).

VAT 12998 MA fragment. Copies: Ebeling, KAR 2, no. 302; Kinnier Wilson Etana, pl. 29.

Abbreviations and Symbols

Bibliographical Abbreviations

79-7-8 etc.	tablets in the collections of the British Museum
AfO	Archiv für Orientforschung
ANET	J. B. Pritchard (ed.), *Ancient Near Eastern Texts Relating to the Old Testament* (3rd edition, Princeton 1969)
ATAT	H. Gressmann, *Altorientalische Texte zum Alten Testament* (Berlin and Leipzig 1926)
BA	Beiträge zur Assyriologie
BRM	Babylonian Records in the Library of J. Pierpont Morgan
CAD	The Assyrian Dictionary of the Oriental Institute of the University of Chicago
Cat. Suppl.	L. W. King, *Catalogue of the Cuneiform Tablets in the Kouyunjik Collection, Supplement* (London 1914)
CT	Cuneiform Texts from Babylonian Tablets in the British Museum
Dalley *Myths*	S. Dalley, *Myths from Mesopotamia* (Oxford 1989)
Haul Etana	M. Haul, *Das Etana-Epos* (Göttingen 2000)
Hunger *Kolophone*	H. Hunger, *Babylonische und assyrische Kolophone* (AOAT 2, Neukirchen 1968)
JAOS	Journal of the American Oriental Society
JNES	Journal of Near Eastern Studies
K	tablets in the collections of the British Museum
KAR	E. Ebeling, *Keilschrifttexte aus Assur religiösen Inhalts* (Leipzig 1919)
KB	Keilinschriftliche Bibliothek
Kinnier Wilson Etana	J.V. Kinnier Wilson, *The Legend of Etana. A New Edition* (Warminster 1985)
Langdon Etana	S. Langdon, *The Legend of Etana and the Eagle, or the Epical Poem "The City they Hated," Babyloniaca* 12 (1931) 1-53, pls. I-XIV
LKA	E. Ebeling and F. Köcher, *Literarische Keilschrifttexte aus Assur* (Berlin 1953)
MLC	tablets in the collections of the J. Pierpont Morgan Library
Or.	Orientalia
RA	Revue d'assyriologie
Rm	tablets in the collections of the British Museum
RT	Recueil de travaux relatifs à la philologie et à l'archéologie égyptiennes et assyriennes
SAA	State Archives of Assyria

SAACT	State Archives of Assyria Cuneiform Texts
SAA Gilg.	S. Parpola, *The Standard Babylonian Epic of Gilgamesh* (SAACT 1)
Saporetti Etana	C. Saporetti, *Etana* (Palermo 1990)
Sm	tablets in the collections of the British Museum
Thompson Gilg.	R.C. Thompson, *The Epic of Gilgamish* (Oxford 1930)
TIM	Texts in the Iraq Museum
VAT	tablets in the collections of the Vorderasiatisches Museum, Berlin
YOR	Yale Oriental Series, Researches

Other Abbreviations and Symbols

MA	Middle Assyrian
NA	Neo-Assyrian
OB	Old Babylonian
SB	Standard Babylonian
e.	edge
obv.	obverse
pl.	plate
r., rev.	reverse
col.	column
coll.	collated, collation
mng.	meaning
ms.	manuscript
unpub.	unpublished
var.	variant
!	collation
!!	emendation
?	uncertain reading
:	cuneiform division mark
*	graphic variants (see LAS I p. XX)
0	uninscribed space or nonexistent sign
x	broken or undeciphered sign
( )	supplied word or sign
(( ))	sign erroneously added by scribe
[[ ]]	erasure
+	joined to
(+)	indirect join

CUNEIFORM TEXT

TABLET I

break of approximately 26 lines

approximately 90 lines destroyed

TABLET II

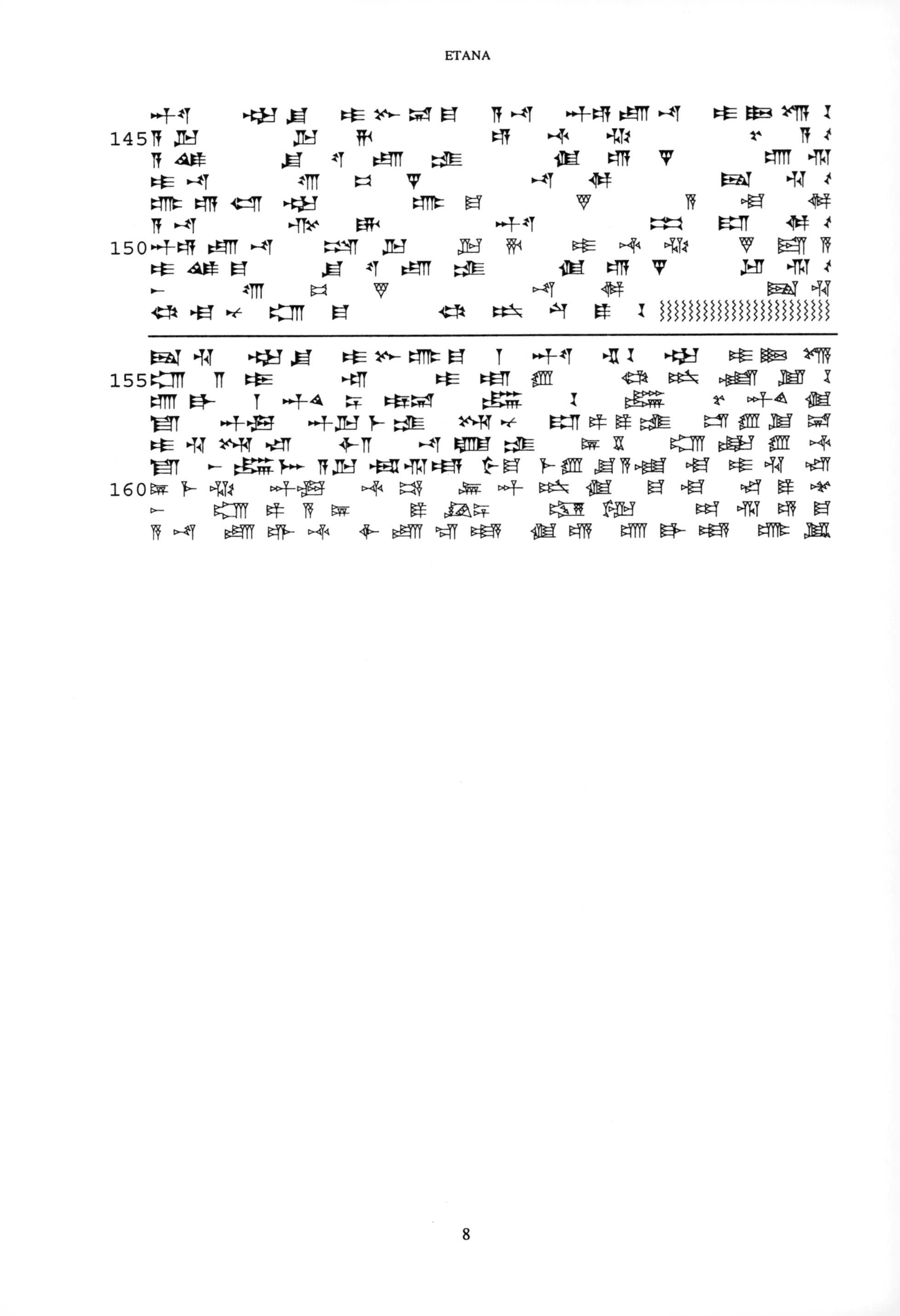

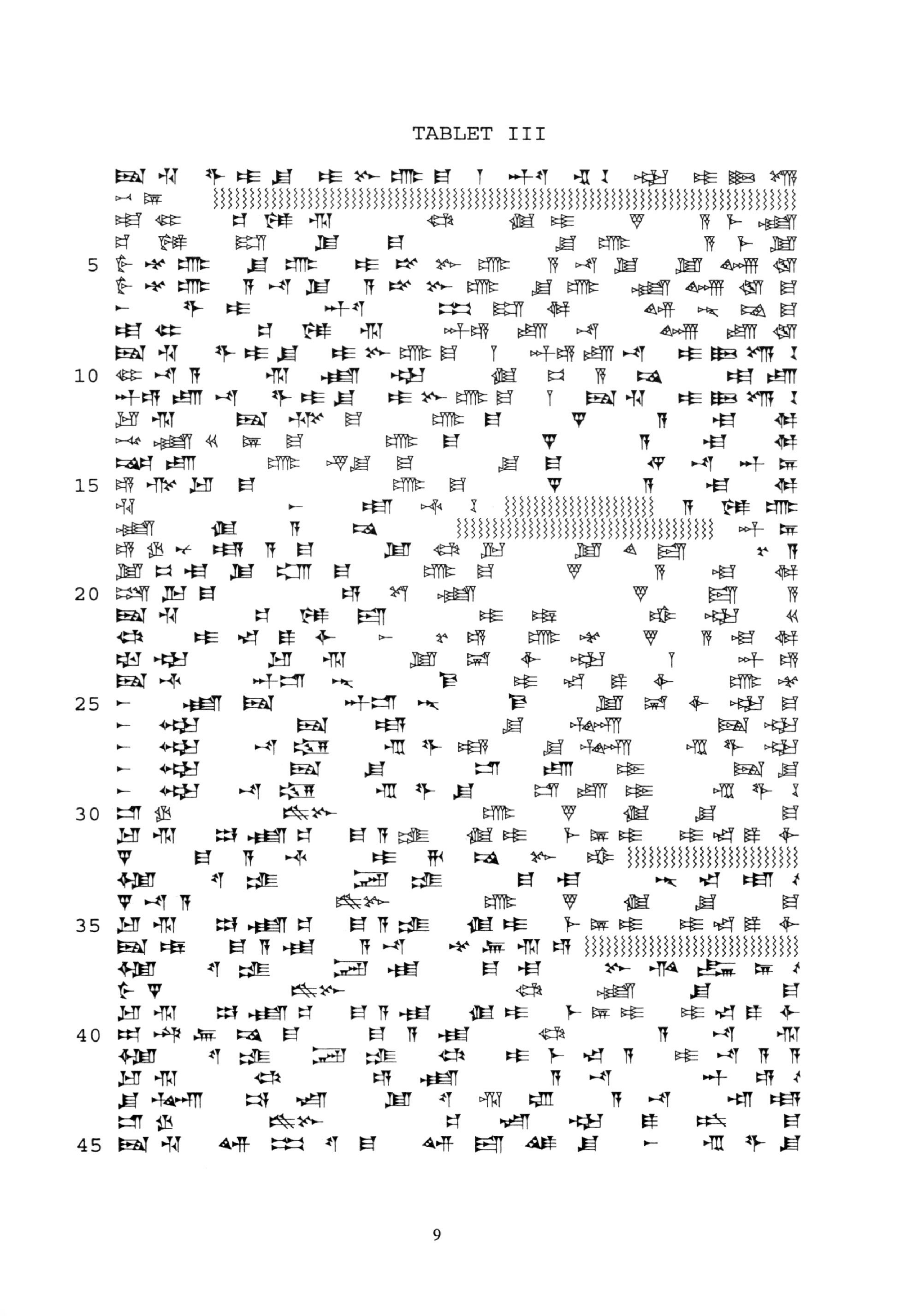

TABLET III

break of approximately 13 lines

break of approximately 7 lines

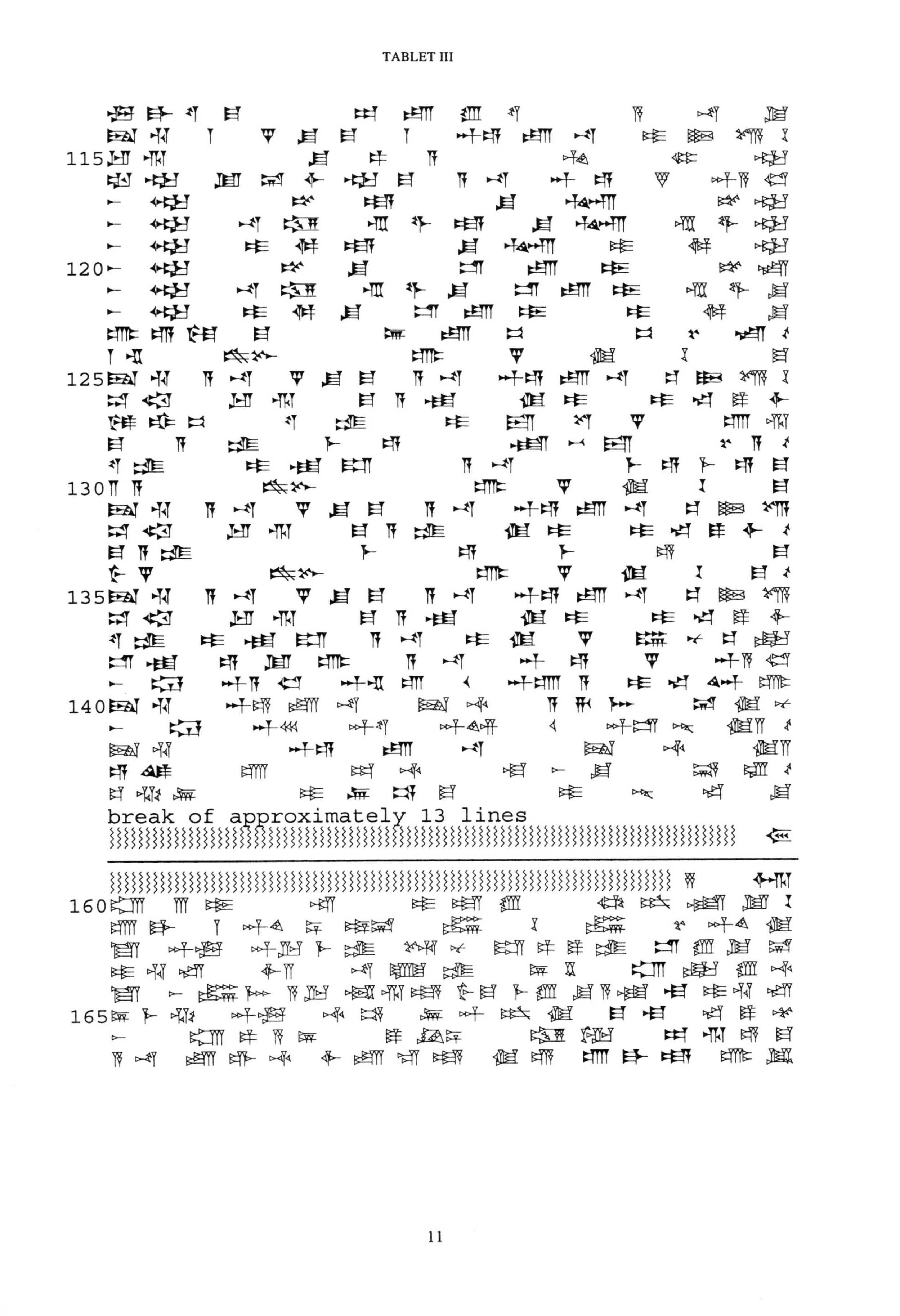

break of approximately 13 lines

K 14788

beginning broken away

rest broken away

TRANSLITERATION

TABLET I

1 URU *i-ṣi-r[u ul-tak?-li?-lu?-šú]*
2 *[uš-ši-šú id]-du-ú* DINGIR.MEŠ [GAL.MEŠ]
3 [KIŠ.K]I *ṣi-(ru)* ⸢*i*⸣*-ṣi-ru* ⸢*ul*⸣*-[tak?-li?-lu?-šú]*
4 *[uš-š]i-šú id-du-ú* DINGIR.MEŠ [GAL.MEŠ]
5 ⸢^{d}5⸣.1.1 *ú-kin-nu lib-na-a[s-su x x x x]*
6 [LUGA]L? *lu-u re-é-um-ši-n[a x x x x x]*
7 *[e-t]a-na lu-u i-*⸢*tin*⸣*-ši-na e-[x x x x x]*
8 *ši-bir-r[u x x x x]*
9 *[r]a-bu-tum* ^{d}*a-nun-na-k[i mu-šim-mu ši-ma-te]*
10 *[uš-b]u im-tal-li-ku mi-lik-šú-nu [šá ma-a-ti]*
11 *[ba-nu]-ú kib-ra-a-ti šá-ki*!!*-[nu ši-kit-ti]*
12 *z[i]-*⸢*ik*⸣*-ri* DÙ*-šú-nu* ^{d}5.⸢1.1⸣ [EZEN *ana*] ⸢UN?⸣.[MEŠ *i-ši-mu*]
13 *l[a] iš-ku-nu* [LU]GA[L UGU UN.MEŠ *a-pa-a-ti*]
14 *i-na* UD*-mi-šu-ma [la ka-aṣ-rat ku-ub-šu me-a-nu]*
15 *ù* GIŠ.PA NA$_4$.ZA.GÌN *[la ṣa-ap-rat]*
16 *la ba-na-a kib-ra-a-ti* 1*-niš [pa-rak-ki]*
17 ^{d}*se-bet-tum* UGU *um-ma-ni ú-di-*⸢*lu*⸣ [KÁ.MEŠ]
18 UGU *da-ád-me ú-di-lu* [KÁ.MEŠ]
19 URU ^{d}5.1.1 *šu-tas-hu-ru [x x x]*
20 ^{d}IŠ.TAR *re-é-a [x x x x]*
21 *ù* LUGAL *i-še-*⸢*ʾi*⸣*-i [x x x x]*
22 ^{d}*in-nin-na re-*⸢*é*⸣*-[a x x x x]*
23 *ù* LUGAL *i-še-[ʾi-i x x x x]*
24 $^{d+}$EN.LÍL *i-ha-aṭ pa-rak-ki* AN-⸢*e*⸣ *[x x x x x x x x x]*
25 *iš-te-né-ʾe-e-ma [x x x x x x x x x]*
26 *ina ma-a-ti* LUGAL *[x x x x x x x x x]*
27 LUGAL*-ú-tu [i-na* AN*-e ú-ri-dam-ma]*
28 *ub-lam-ma [x x x x x x x x x]*
29 DINGIR.MEŠ KUR.[MEŠ *x x x x x x x x*]
30 *[x]x šu x[x x x x x x x x x x]*

break of approximately 26 lines

57 *[x x] nu x[x x x x x x x x x]*
58 *[mar]-hi-is-su ana šá-šu-m[a ana e-ta-ni i-zak-kar-šú]*
59 *[šu-u]t-tu ia-a-ši ú-*⸢*šab*⸣*-[ra-an-ni* ^{d}*x x x]*
60 GIM *e-ta-ni mu-ti* ⸢*ku*?⸣ *x[x x x x x x x]*
61 GIM *ka-a-ši [x x x x x x x]*
62 ⸢^{d}⸣*e-ta-na šar-*⸢*ru*⸣ *x[x x x x x x x x]*
63 *e-ṭém-mu-šu ana [x]x [x x x x x x]*
64 *ù la* ⸢*ud*?⸣ [x] ⸢*ina*? É? *x x x*⸣ *x[x x x x x x]*
65 *zu x[x x x x x]x ma x[x x x x x]*
66 ⸢UGU *mu-ut*⸣ *[x x x x x]* ⸢*x x*⸣ *[x x x x x]*

approximately 90 lines destroyed

---

155 *[x-da a-me-lu* MU*-šú i-nam?-x x x x]*
156 [DUB 1.KÁM URU *i-ṣi-ru ul-tak?-li?-lu?-šú*]
157 [É.GAL ^{m}AN.ŠÁR—DÙ—DUMU.UŠ LUGAL ŠÚ LUGAL KUR—AN.ŠÁR.KI]
158 *[ša* ^{d}AG ^{d}*taš-me-tum uz-nu ra-pa-áš-tum iš-ru-ku-uš]*
159 *[i-hu-zu* IGI.2 *na-mir-tum ni-siq ṭup-šar-ru-ti]*
160 *[ša ina* LUGAL.MEŠ *a-lik mah-ri-ia mám-ma šip-ru šu-a-tu la i-hu-zu]*
161 *[né-me-eq* ^{d}AG *ti-kip sa-an-tak-ki ma-la ba-áš-mu]*
162 *[ina ṭup-pa-a-ni áš-ṭur as-niq ab-re-e-ma]*
163 *[a-na ta-mar-ti ši-ta-si-ia qé-reb* É.GAL*-ia ú-kin]*

I 1 *ul-tak-li-lu-šú*: restoration SP, conjectural, cf. line 3 (*ul-*), colophon of Tablet III (*-šú*), and CAD s.v. *šuklulu*; possibly also *ul-te-eṣ-bu-u-šú*, cf. CAD s.v. *ṣubbû* 2, 4 MEŠ shown as preserved in Langdon's copy 6 [LUGA]L?: traces would also fit [L]Ú. However, "man" is elsewhere in the epic written syllabically. 8 Erasure before *ši-* 9 OB$_M$: *ra-bu-tum* ^{d}A.NUN.NA *ša-i-mu ši-im-tim*; for restoration cf. CAD Š/1 362 10-17 Restored from OB$_M$ 11 *ki*!!: tablet IM 27 Restoration conjectural, cf. OB$_M$ i 14

TABLET II

1 *[x]x-da a-me-lu* MU-*šú i-n[am*$^{?}$*-x x x x x x x]*
2 *[di]-in-ta i-te-pu-uš [x x x x x x x]*
3 *[p]a-rak-ki šá* ^{d}IM DINGIR-*šu [x x x x x x x]*
4 *ina* GIŠ.MI *pa-rak-ki šá-a-šú a-ṣa-at ṣa[r-ba-tu e-li-tu]*
5 *ina ap-pi-šá ra-bi-iṣ* Á.MUŠEN *[ina iš-di-šá ka-nin* MUŠ]
6 ⸢UD⸣-*mi-šam-ma i-na-ṣ[a-ru a-ha-meš]*
7 ⸢Á⸣.MUŠEN KA-*šu i-pu-šam-m[a a-na* MUŠ *i-zak-kar-šú]*
8 *[al]-ka ni-⸢nu-u-ma ru-u_8⸣-a-[u-tu i ni-pu-uš]*
9 *⸢lu-u⸣ it-ba-ru a-n[a-ku u at-ta]*
10 [MUŠ] KA-*šu i-pu-šam-ma [a-na* Á.MUŠEN *i-zak-kar-šú]*
11 [^{d}UTU$^{?}$ *š]u-⸢u⸣ šá ru-u_8-a-u-tu x[x x x x x x x]*
12 *le[m-né-t]a-ma kab-t[a-as-su tu-šam-ra-aṣ]*
13 *an-z[il-la] šá* DINGIR.MEŠ *[a-sak-ka ta-kal]*
14 *al-⸢ka⸣ ni-zaq-pa-am-ma [šá-da-a ni-li]*
15 *ni-it-ma-a* KI-*tim* [DAGAL-*tim*]
16 *ina ma-har* ^{d}UTU *qu-ra-di ma-mit it-[mu-ú]*
17 *[šá] i-ta-a šá* ^{d}UTU *[it-ti-qu]*
18 ^{d}UTU *lem-niš ina qa-at ma-hi-ṣ[i li-mal-li]*
19 *šá i-ta-a šá* ^{d}UTU *[it-ti-qu]*
20 *li-is-su-šu-ma né-re-[bé-ti šá* KUR-*e*]
21 GIŠ.TUKUL *mur-tap-pi-du* UGU-*šu [li-še-er]*
22 *giš-par-ru ma-mit* ^{d}UTU *lib-bal-ki-tu-šu-ma l[i-ba-ru-šu]*
23 *iš-tu ma-mit it-mu-ú* KI-*t[im* DAGAL-*tim*]
24 *iz-zaq-pu-nim-ma šá-da-a e-lu-⸢ú⸣*
25 UD-1-KÁM-TA.ÀM *i-na-ṣa-ru* MÁ[Š.ANŠE]
26 GUD.AM *sír-ri-mu* Á.MUŠEN *i-bar-ra[m-ma]*
27 MUŠ *ik-kal i-né-e*ʾ*-ú ik-ka-lu* DUMU.MEŠ-*[šú]*
28 *ar-mi* MAŠ.DÀ.MEŠ MUŠ *i-bar-ram-[ma]*
29 Á.MUŠEN *ik-kal i-né-e*ʾ*-ú ik-ka-lu* DUMU.MEŠ-*[šú]*
30 *sa-ap-pa-ri di-da-ni* Á.MUŠEN *i-bar-ram-m[a]*
31 MUŠ *ik-kal i-né-e*ʾ*-ú ik-ka-lu* DUMU.MEŠ-*[šú]*
32 [MÁ]Š.ANŠ[E EDIN *nam-maš]-ti qaq-qa-ri* MUŠ *i-bar-ram-m[a]*
33 [Á.MUŠEN *ik-kal i]-⸢né⸣-e*ʾ*-ú ik-ka-lu* DUMU.MEŠ-⸢*šú*⸣
34 ⸢DUMU.MEŠ⸣ [Á.MUŠEN *i-ku-lu*] ⸢*ú*⸣*-kul-ta* :
35 DUMU.M[EŠ] Á.MUŠEN *ir-bu-u i-ši-hu*
36 *iš-tu* DUMU.MEŠ ⸢Á.MUŠEN⸣ *ir-bu-ú i-ši-hu*
37 Á.MUŠEN ŠÀ-*ba-šu le-mut-tu ik-pu-du-m[a]*
38 *ik-pu-ud-ma* ŠÀ-*ba-šu le-mut-tu*
39 *a-na at-mi šá ru-u_8-a-šú a-ka-li p[a-ni]-šú iš-kun*
40 Á.MUŠEN KA-*šu i-pu-uš-ma i-zak-kar ⸢a⸣-[na* DUMU.MEŠ-*šú*]
41 DUMU.MEŠ MUŠ-*mi lu-ku-lu ana-ku* :
42 MUŠ-*mi* ⸢ŠÀ⸣-*[ba-šú i-mar-ra-aṣ]*
43 *e-li-ma i-na šá-ma-mi uš-[šab]*
44 *ur-rad i-na ap-pi iṣ-ṣi-ma a-kal in-⸢ba⸣*
45 *at-mu ṣe-eh-ru a-tar ha-si-sa* :
46 *a-na* Á.MUŠEN AD-*šú* INIM M[U]-*ár*
47 *la ta-kal a-bi še-e-tu šá* ^{d}UTU *i-ba-á[r-ka]*
48 *giš-par-ru ma-mit* ^{d}UTU *ib-bal-ki-tu-ka-ma i-bar-ru-⸢nik⸣-k[a]*
49 *šá i-ta-a šá* ^{d}UTU *it-ti-qu* :
50 ^{d}UTU *lem-niš ina qa-at [ma-hi-ṣi ú-mal-la]*
51 *ul iš-me-šu-nu-ti-ma ul iš-ma-a [zi-kir* DU]MU.M[EŠ-*šú*]
52 ⸢*ú*⸣*-ri-dam-ma e-ta-kal* DUMU.[MEŠ MUŠ]
53 *ina ⸢li-la⸣-a-ti ina qer-bit* UD-*me* :
54 MUŠ *il-[li-kam-ma]* U[ZU *i-n]a-ši bi-lat-su* :
55 *ina* KÁ *qin-ni-[šu* UZU *it-ta-di]*
56 *[ip-pal]-⸢sa⸣-ma qin-na-šú la-áš-šú* :
57 *ú-ši-ir-ma ul [x x x x x]*
58 *[ṣú-up]-ra-nu-uš-šú qaq-qa-ra [x x x x]*
59 *e-l[e-n]u tur-bu-u*ʾ*-ta-šú šá-ma-m[i i-qat-tur]*
60 MUŠ *i-n[a]-⸢*ʾ*i*$^{?}$⸣*-il-ma i-bak-ki* :
61 *a-na pa-an* ^{d}UTU *i[l-la-ka di-ma-a-šú]*
62 *at-kal-kúm-ma* ^{d}UTU *[qu-ra-du]*
63 *a-na* Á.MUŠEN Z[ÍD.MUNU$_4$] ⸢*a-na*⸣*-k[u áš-ru-uk]*
64 *e-nen-na qin-ni [da-ma-míš i-me]*
65 *qin-ni ia-ú la*$^{?}$*-áš*$^{?}$*-[š]u*$^{?}$ ⸢*qin*⸣*-[na-šú šá-li-im]*

II 4 *e-li-tu*: restoration SP, conjectural 5 Restoration SP, conjectural, cf. MA_1 6 Restoration SP, conjectural 11 Restoration SP, conjectural 12f Restored from line 130f 14f Restored from line 23f 17, 19 Restored from line 49 18 Restored from MA_1; cf. line 50 20 OBS: *li-ik-la-šu ne-re-eb-ta-šu šà-du-ú* 22 Restored from line 48; cf. OBS 32 Restored from MA_1 42 Restoration SP; cf. MA_1 50 For restoration cf. note on line 18 51 F has : between *-š]u-nu-ti-ma* and *ul* 53 ⸢*ina*$^{?}$ *li*$^{?}$*-la*$^{?}$⸣*-a-ti* B_2 : *li-la-tu* OBS 56 *i-na* F 55 OBS: *ip-pa-li-is-ma la-aš-šu-ú* [...] 58 Restored from OBS 59 Restoration SP, conjectural, cf. SAA Gilg IV 168; another possibility is *šá-ma-*

66 sa-ap-hu at-mu-ú-a ša[l-mu at-mu-ú-šú]
67 ú-ri-dam-ma e-ta-kal [li-da-ni-ia]
68 ⸢lum⸣-nu šá i-pu-šá-an-ni ^{d}U[TU lu ti-di]
69 a-bar-šá ^{d}UTU še-et-ka er-ṣe-[tum DAGAL-tum]
70 giš-par-ru-ka AN-ú [ru-qu-tu]
71 i-na še-ti-ka a-a ú-ṣ[i Á.MUŠEN]
72 e-piš HUL-tim an-zu-ú mu-kil [HUL-tim ana ib-ri-šú]
73 un-né-ni šá MUŠ [i-na še-mi-šu]
74 ^{d}UTU KA-šu i-pu-šá-am-ma a-n[a MUŠ i-zak-kar-šú]
75 a-lik ur-ha e-ti-i[q šá-da-a]
76 ⸢uk⸣-ta-as-si-ka ri-[mu]
77 [pe]-te-e-ma ŠÀ-ba-šu [ka-ra-as-su šu-ṭu-uṭ]
78 ⸢šu-ub⸣-ta id-di [ina kar-ši-šú]
79 [mim-mu-ú] iṣ-ṣu-rat šá-ma-mì [ur-ra-da-ma ik-ka-la UZU]
80 [Á.MU]ŠEN it-ti-ši-n[a ik-ka-al UZU]
81 [ki?] la i-du-ú-⸢ma a⸣-n[a x x x x x]
82 nu-ru-ub UZU iš-te-né-e'-i sa-da-a-ti it-ta-na-al-lak
83 a-na ku-tu-um ŠÀ-bi uš-ta-ma-a[ṣ-ṣ]a
84 a-na ŠÀ-bi ina e-re-bi-šu at-ta ṣa-bat-su i-[n]a kap-pi-šú
85 nu-uk-kis kap-pi-šu ab-ri-šú ù n[u-bal-l]i-šú
86 bu-qu-un-šu-ma i-di-šú ana šu-ut-ta-⸢ti ša la $^{d!}$UTU$^{!}$⸣-ši
87 mu-ut bu-bu-ti ù ṣu-um-mi ⸢li-mu-ta⸣
88 a-na zi-kir ^{d}UTU qu-ra-di :
89 MUŠ il-lik i-ti-iq šá-⸢da⸣-a
90 ik-šu-ud-ma MUŠ a-na ṣe-e[r ri]-mi
91 ip-te-e-ma ŠÀ-ba-šú ka-ra-as-s[u iš]-ṭu-uṭ
92 šu-ub-ta id-di i-na kar-ši-šú
93 mim-mu-ú iṣ-ṣu-rat šá-ma-mì ú-[ri]-da-ma ik-ka-la ši-i-ra
94 Á.MUŠEN lu-mu-un-šú i-[d]a-a-ma
95 it-ti DUMU.MEŠ iṣ-ṣu-ri ul ik-kal ši-i-ra
96 Á.MUŠEN pa-a-šu i-pu-šá-am-ma i-zak-ka-ra ana DUMU.MEŠ-šú
97 [al]-ka-nim-ma i ni-rid-ma UZU AM an-né-e i ni-ku-la ni-nu
98 [at]-mu ṣe-eh-ru a-tar ha-si-sa [:]
99 [a-na Á.MUŠEN AD-šú a]-ma-tum i-zak-kar
100 [la tu]r-rad a-bi mìn-de ina ⸢ŠÀ⸣-bi ⸢AM⸣ an-né-e MUŠ ra-bi-iṣ
101 ⸢Á⸣.MUŠEN it-ti ⸢ŠÀ-bi-šú a⸣-ma-tum i-qab-bi
102 [iṣ-ṣ]u-ra-a-⸢tu x x⸣-ti ⸢x⸣ [x x].MEŠ ki-i-mi ik-ka-la š[i-ra]
103 [u]l iš-me-[šú]-nu-ti-ma ul iš-ma-a zi-kir DUM[U.MEŠ]-šú
104 ú-⸢ri-dam⸣-ma it-ta-ziz ina UGU ri-me
105 Á.MUŠEN ⸢ip-ta⸣-qid UZU :
106 iš-te-né-e'-i šá pa-ni-šú ù ár-[k]i-šú
107 iš-ni-i' ip-ta-qid UZU
108 iš-te-né-e'-i šá pa-ni-šú ù ár-[k]i-šú
109 sa-da-a-ti [it]-ta-na-al-lak :
110 a-na ku-⸢tùm⸣ ŠÀ-bi uš-ta-ma-⸢aṣ⸣-ṣa
111 a-na Š[À-b]i ina e-re-bi-šú :
112 MUŠ iṣ-ṣa-bat-su ina kap-pi-šú
113 TU-ub KU-NE-en-ni TU-ub KU-NE-en-ni
114 Á.MUŠEN K[A-šu] i-pu-šá-am-ma a-na MUŠ i-zak-kar-šú
115 ARHUŠ-an-ni-ma GIM e-re-ši nu-dun-na-a lud-din-ka
116 MUŠ KA-šu i-pu-šá-am-ma a-na Á.MUŠEN i-zak-[ka]r-šú
117 ú-maš-šar-ka-ma ^{d}UTU e-le-nu ki-i ap-pal
118 še-ret-ka i-sah-hu-ra a-na UGU-hi-ia
119 šá a-šak-ka-nu-ka a-na-ku še-er-ta
120 ú-nak-ki-is kap-pi-šú ab-ri-šú nu-bal-⸢li⸣-šú
121 [ib-qu-u]n-šu-ma id-[di-šu i-na] ⸢šu-ut⸣-[ta-ti]
122 [mu-ut] bu-bu-t[i ù ṣu-mi]-i i-ma-[ta]
123 [Á.MUŠEN ina šu-ut-ta]-⸢ti⸣ [na-di-m]a
124 ⸢UD⸣-mì-šam-ma im-da-na-ha-ra ^{d}UTU
125 [i]-na šu-ut-ta-ti a-ma-ta-ma :
126 man-nu i-di ki-i šak-na-ku še-ret-ka
127 [i]a-a-ši Á.MUŠEN bul-liṭ-an-ni-ma
128 [a-n]a UD-mi da-ru-ú-ti zi-kir-ka lu-uš-te-eš-me
129 ^{d}UTU KA-šú DÙ-uš-ma a-na Á.MUŠEN i-zak-kar-šú
130 lem-né-ta-ma kab-ta-ti tu-šam-ri-iṣ
131 an-zil-la šá DINGIR.MEŠ a-sak-ku ta-ku[l]
132 ta-ma-ta-a-ma la a-sa-an-ni-qa-ak-ka
133 a-lik a-me-la šá a-šap-pa-rak-ka ŠU-ka li-iṣ-bat
134 ^{d}e-ta-na UD-mì-šam-ma im-ta-ah-ha-ra ^{d}UTU-ši
135 ta-kul ^{d}UTU ku-bur šu-'e-e-a :
136 KI-tum taš-ti-i da-am as-li-ia

mi-[iš i-li], see CAD s.v. šamû A 1a 61ff Restored from OB_S 65 For restoration cf. OB_S 67-72 Restored from OB_S 75 Restored from line 89 and 145 76-80 Restored from lines 90-95 82 Written on two separate lines on G 82-84 Cf. lines 109-112 84 ina F : i-na G; written on two separate lines on G 85-87 Cf. lines 120-122 85 Restored from line 120; kap-pi-šú G : -šu F 86 bu-qu-un-šú-ma G : -šu-ma F; id-di G : i-di-šú F; $^{d!}$UTU$^{!}$-ši: reading after SP 87 ṣu-mi G : ṣu-um-[mi F 88 qu-⸢ra-du⸣ G : -di F; G omits ":" since lines 88-89 are there written on two separate lines 92 id-di F : it-ta-di G 93 šá-ma-mì F : -mi G; written on two separate lines on G 96 pa-a-šu F : ⸢KA⸣-šu B_2; i-pu-šá-am-ma B_2 : i-pu-šam-ma G 98f written on two separate lines on F 101 a-ma-tu B_2 : -tum G 102 written on two separate lines on F 104 ri-me B_2 : -mi F 104f written on a single line on F, with ri-mi and Á separated by : 105f written on a single line on B_2 without : 107 division marker : written after UZU on F 107f written on a single line on B_2 without : 109f written on a single line on B_2 without : 111 e-re-bi-šú B_2 : -šu F 113 or read as KU_4-ub tuš-pel en-ni 121f Restored from lines 86f 123 Restoration SP; cf. line 147 124 Cf. line 134 130f Cf. line 12f 131 ta-ku[l] B_3 : -k]u-⸢ul⸣ G 133 a-lik B_3 : a-l[i-ik G 134]-ši G; cf. line 124 135 G omits : since lines 135-136

137 DINGIR.MEŠ *ú-kab-bit e-ṭém-me ap-làh*
138 *ig-dam-ra maš-šak-ki-ia* MÍ.EN.ME.LI.MEŠ
139 *as-li-ia ina ṭu-ub-bu-hi* DINGIR.MEŠ *ig-dam-ru*
140 *be-lum ina pi-i-ka li-ṣa-am-ma* :
141 *id-nam-ma šam-ma šá a-la-di*
142 *kul-li-man-ni-ma šam-ma šá a-la-di* :
143 *pil-ti ú-suh-ma šu-ma šuk-na-an-ni*
144 ^{d}UTU KA-*šu i-pu-uš-ma a-na* ^{d}*e-ta-na i-zak-kar-šú*
145 *a-lik ur-ha e-ti-iq* KUR-*a* :
146 *a-mur šu-ut-ta-tum qé-reb-šá bit-ri*
147 *i-na* ŠÀ-*bi-šá na-di* Á.MUŠEN :
148 *ú-kal-lam-ka šam-m[a šá a-la-d]i*
149 *a-na zi-kir* ^{d}UTU *qu-ra-di* :
150 ^{d}*e-ta-na il-lik [ur-ha i-ti-iq šá-da-a]*
151 *i-mur-ma šu-ut-ta-tum qé-reb-šá ib-ri* :
152 *ina* ŠÀ-[*bi-šá na-di* Á.MUŠEN]
153 *ul-la-nu-um-ma ul-taq-qa-áš-š[ú x x x x]*

---

154 Á.MUŠEN KA-*šu i-pu-šam-ma ana* ^{d}UTU EN-*šú* INIM [*i-zak-kar*]
155 DUB 2.KÁM URU *i-ṣi-r[u ul-tak?-li?-lu?-šú]*
156 É.GAL ^{m}AN.ŠÁR—DÙ—DUMU.UŠ LUGAL ŠÚ [LUGAL KUR—AN.ŠÁR.KI]
157 *ša* ^{d}AG ^{d}*taš-me-tum uz-nu ra-p[a-áš-tum iš-ru-ku-uš]*
158 *i-hu-uz-zu* IGI.2 *na-mir-tum [ni-siq ṭup-šar-ru-ti]*
159 *ša ina* LUGAL.MEŠ *a-lik mah-ri-ia mám-[ma šip-ru šu-a-tu la i-hu-zu]*
160 [*né-me-eq* ^{d}AG *ti-kip sa-an-tak-ki ma-la ba-áš-mu*]
161 [*ina ṭup-pa-a-ni áš-ṭur as-niq ab-re-e-ma*]
162 [*a-na ta-mar-ti ši-ta-si-ia qé-reb* É.GAL-*ia ú-kin*]

are written on two separate lines 136 KI-*tum* B_3 : *er-ṣe-t[um* G 139 *ina* B_3 : *i-na* G 140 *be-lum* B_3 : *-lí* G; *ina* B_3 : *i-na* G; G omits ":" since lines 140-141 are there written on two separate lines 141ff Cf. III 12ff 142 G omits : since lines 142-143 are written on two separate lines 144 KA-*šu* B_3 : *pi-i-šú* G; *i-pu-uš-ma* B_3 : *i-pu-*⌜*šam-ma*⌝ G; ^{d}*e-ta-na* B_3 : ^{m}*e-ta-na* G 145 KUR-*a* B_3 : *šá-da-a* G; G omits ":" since lines 145-146 are there written on two separate lines; cf. line 75 147 Á.MUŠEN B_3 : ⌜*e*⌝*-ru-ú* G; B omits ":" since lines 147-148 are there written on two separate lines 148 Restored from line 142 153 *ul-taq-qa-á[š-šú* B_3 : *uš-ta-qa-áš-š[ú* A 154f Lines reversed on A 154 KA-*šu* B_3 : *pi-i-šu* A; *ana* B_3 : *a-na* A 155 DUB 2.KÁM B_3 : DUB 3.KÁM A

TABLET III

1 Á.MUŠEN *pi-i-šu i-pu-šam-ma ana* ^{d}UTU EN-*šú* [INIM *i-zak-kar*]

2 [*be-l*]*í x*[*x*] *x*[*x x x x x x x x x*]

3 [*at-m*]*i iṣ-ṣu-ri* [*ul ki-i šá a-me-li*]

4 [*iṣ-ṣu-r*]*a-ku-ma* [*šu-ú a-me-lu*]

5 [*mim*]-*mu-ú šu-ú i-qab-b*[*u-ú a-na-ku lu-uh-kim*]

6 [*mi*]*m-mu-ú a-na-ku a-qab-bu-*[*ú šu-ú li-ih-kim-ma*]

7 *ina pi-i* ^{d}UTU *qu-r*[*a-di im-qut-am-ma*]

8 *at-mi iṣ-ṣu-ri* [^{d}*e-ta-na ih-ta-kim*]

9 Á.MUŠEN *pi-i-šu i-pu-š*[*am-ma ana* ^{d}*e-t*]*a-na i-zak-kar-šú*

10 [*mi*]-*na-a tal-li-ka* [*qí-bi*]-⸢*a*⸣-*am at-ta*

11 ^{d}*e-ta-na pi-i-šu i-pu-ša*[*m-ma ana*] Á.MUŠEN *i-zak-kar-šú*

12 ⸢*ib*⸣-*ri id-nam-*⸢*ma*⸣ [*ša*]*m-ma šá a-la-di*

13 ⸢*kul-li-man*⸣-*n*[*i-ma š*]*am-ma šá a-la-di*

14 *pil-ta* [*ú-suh-ma š*]*u-ma šuk-na-an-ni*

15 ⸢*e*⸣-*zi-ib-ma* [*šam-m*]*a šá a-la-di*

16 [MUŠ]EN? *ina ṣi-t*[*i-šú x*]*x a-ṣu-ú*

17 ⸢*le*?⸣-*qé-a-am* [*x x x-a*]*n-ni*

18 [*e-d*]*in-nu-ia-a-ma l*[*u-ul-lik lu-hi-ṭa*] KUR-*a*

19 [*lu*]-*bi-la-ku-um-ma* [*šam-ma šá a*]-⸢*la-di*⸣

20 [*i*]*l-lik-ma e-*[*te-li šá-da-a*]

21 Á.MUŠEN *iṣ-ṣu-da* [*i-tur ár-ka-niš*]

22 *ul i-ba-áš-ši* [*ina* KUR-*e šam-mu šá a-la-di*]

23 *al-ka ib-ri* [*lu-uš-ši-ka ana* AN-*e*]

24 *it-ti* ^{d}IŠ.TAR GAŠAN [*i-ba-áš-ši šam-mu*]

25 *ina le-et* ^{d}IŠ.TAR GAŠAN [*lu-uš-ši-ka-ma*]

26 *ina* UGU Á-*ia* [*šu-kun* Á-*ka*]

27 *ina* UGU *na-aṣ kap-pi-i*[*a šu-kun kap-pi-ka*]

28 *ina* UGU Á-*šu iš-ta-ka*[*n* Á-*šu*]

29 *ina* UGU *na-aṣ kap-pi-šu* [*iš-ta-kan kap-pi-šú*]

30 *iš-t*[*in*] KASKAL.GÍD [*ú-šá-qí-šu-ma*]

31 *ib-ri nap-li-is ma-a-t*[*um*] ⸢*ki*⸣-[*i mì-ni-i i-ba-áš-ši*]

32 *šá ma-a-ti i-ha-am-b*[*u-ub x x x*]

33 *ù tam-tum* DAGAL-*tum ma-la tar-ba-ṣi* :

34 *šá-na-a* KASK[AL.GÍD *ú-šá-qí-šu-ma*]

35 *ib-ri nap-li-is ma-a-tum ki-i* [*mì-ni-i i-ba-áš-ši*]

36 *it-tur ma-a-tu a-na mu-sa-re-e x*[*x x x x x*]

37 *ù tam-tum* DAGAL-*tu ma-la bu-gi-in-ni* :

38 *šal-šá* KASKAL.GÍD [*u*]*l-*⸢*li*⸣-*šu-ma*

39 *ib-ri nap-li-is ma-a-tu ki-i mì-n*[*i-i*] ⸢*i*⸣-*ba-áš-ši*

40 *ap-pal-sa-am-ma ma-a-tu u*[*l*] *a-na-ṭal*

41 *ù tam-tum* DAGAL-*tum ul i-šeb-ba-a* ⸢*i*⸣-*na-a-a*

42 *ib-ri ul e-li a-na* AN-*e* :

43 *šu-kun kib-su lu-ut-*[*t*]*al-lak a-na* URU-*ia*

44 *iš-tin* KASKAL.GÍD *is-su-ka-áš-šum-ma*

45 Á.MUŠEN *im-qu-ut-ma im-da-har-šu ina kap-pi-šu*

46 *šá-na-a* KASKAL.GÍD *is-su-ka-áš-šum-ma*

47 Á.MUŠEN *im-qu-ut-ma im-da-har-šu ina* [*kap*]-⸢*pi*⸣-*šu*

48 *šal-šá* KASKAL.GÍD *is-s*[*u-ka-áš-šum-m*]*a*

49 Á.MUŠEN *im-qu-ut-ma im-da-har-*[*šu ina kap-pi-šu*]

50 [*n*]*ik-kàs a-na qaq-qa-ri* [*is-su-ka-áš-šum-ma*]

51 [Á].MUŠEN *im-qu-ut-ma im-d*[*a-har-šu ina kap-pi-šu*]

52 [*x x-m*]*a* Á.MUŠEN *i-tar-rak* :

53 *šá e-t*[*a-na x x x x x x x x*]

54 [*x x x*]*x x*[*x x x x x x x x x*]

55 [*x x x*] *lak ka ta* [*x x x x x x x x x x*]

56 [*x x x x x*] ⸢*x x*⸣ [*x x x x x x x x x*]

break of approximately 13 lines

70 [*x x x al-k*]*a-ma x*[*x x*] ⸢*dam*⸣ [*x x x*]

71 [*x x x*]*x* ⸢*e*⸣-*ta-*⸢*nap-pal*⸣-[*k*]*a*

72 [*x x x x x x*] ⸢*ú*?⸣-*tab-bi-ku-šú* :

73 *ik-šud-ma* ⸢URU⸣-*šu u* É-*su*

74 [Á.MUŠEN *ana šá-šu-ma*] *ana* ^{d}⸢*e-ta*⸣-*ni i-zak-kar-šu*

75 [*x x x x x*] *šam-mu šá a-la-di*

76 [*x x x*]*x te-qí-tu*

77 [*x x x x*]-*mu-ra ṣi-is-su*

78 [*x x x x x*] *ana k*[*a*]-*šá li-ih-*⸢*di*⸣

79 [Á.MUŠEN *ana šá-šu-ma*] *ana* ⸢^{d}⸣*e-*⸢*ta*⸣-*ni i-*[*zak-kar-šu*]

80 [*x x x x x x*] ⸢*x*⸣ [*x x*] *x*[*x x x*]

81 [*x x x x x x*] ⸢*x*⸣ [*x x x x x*]

82 [*x x x x x x*] ⸢*x an*⸣ *šu ki*? *x*[*x x*]

83 [*x x x x x x x*] *ul ib-*[*ši*?]

84 [*x x x x x x it*?-*t*]*a*?-*ṣi* MU.AN.⸢NA?⸣

III 3 Restoration SP, conjectural 7 Restoration SP, conjectural; cf. II 140 12ff Restored from II 141ff 18 Restoration SP, conjectural 21-25 Restorations SP, conjectural 26f Restored from lines 28f and 118f 30 Restored from line 124; [1-*en*] 1.KASKAL.GÍD N : *iš-t*[*in* O 31 ⸢*nap-li-is*⸣ *ma-a-t*[*um*] M : *nap-lis-ma ma-*⸢*a-tú*⸣ N; cf. line 35 32 Or read as *i-ha-am-mu*[*š*] 33 *tam-tum* M : -⸢*tu*⸣ N 34 KASKA[L.GÍD O : 1.KASKAL.G[ÍD N 35 *nap-li-is ma-a-tum* M : *nap-li-is-*⸢*ma ma-a*⸣-*tu* N 36 *it-tur* MO : -*tu-ru* N 37 *tam-tum* MO : -*tu* N 43 Cf. line 73 48-51 Restored from line 46f 52 Or read as *i-haš-šal* 70-78 Readings suggested by SP 73 Cf. line 43 74, 79 Or restore

85 [x x x x x x] ik-šu-dam-ma [x x]
86 [x x x x x x x]x pa-ni-šú iš-ku[n]
87 [x x x x x x x]-šú i-pa-šar
88 [x x x x x x ma-t]um me-e-me-e-ma
89 [x x x x x x x x x x x]x-bi
90 [x x x x x x x x x x x]x-ma
91 [x x x x x x x x x x x]x ⸢È⸣
92 [x x x x x x x x x x x] ⸢x⸣
break of approximately 7 lines
100 ⸢^{d}e⸣-[ta-na] pi-[i]-⸢šu DÙ⸣-[uš-ma ana Á.MUŠEN i-zak-kar-šú]
101 i[b-ri ú-šab-r]a-a DINGIR ⸢šu⸣-u-⸢ma⸣ [šu-ut-ta]
102 ⸢né⸣-reb šá KÁ ^{d}a-nim $^{d+}$EN.LÍ[L ù] ^{d}É.[A n]i-ba-ʾu-⸢ú⸣
103 nu-uš-ke-nu [a-n]a-ku u at-[ta]
104 ⸢né⸣-reb šá KÁ ^{d}30 ^{d}UTU ^{d}IM u ^{d}⸢IŠ.TAR⸣ ni-ba-ʾu-⸢ú⸣
105 [nu-uš-ke-nu] a-na-ku u at-[ta]
106 a-mur É ap-ti l[a-áš-šu] NA$_4$.KIŠIB [0]
107 ⸢GIŠ.IG⸣-[s]a a-sa-kip-ma e-tar-ba-áš-[šu]
108 áš-bat ina ŠÀ-bi 1-et [KI.SIKIL]
109 ⸢AGA⸣ ru-uṣ-ṣu-na-at DÙ [M]ÚŠ-[šá]
110 GIŠ.GU.ZA ŠUB-ma DINGIR-u-[tú š]u$^{?}$-taq-ba-[at$^{?}$]
111 ina šap-la GIŠ.GU.ZA la-b[e] rab-[ṣu]
112 at-be-ma a-na-ku la-be i[š-taḫ-ṭu-(ni)]
113 ag-gal-tam-ma ap-ta-ru-u[d a-na-ku$^{?}$]
114 Á.MUŠEN ana šá-šu-ma ana ^{d}e-ta-na [i-zak-kar-šú]
115 ib$^{!!}$-ri šu-pa-a MÁ[Š.MI-ka]
116 al-ka lu-uš-ši-ka-ma a-na AN-e [šá ^{d}a-nim]
117 ina UGU GABA-ia šu-kun [GABA-ka]
118 ina UGU na-aṣ kap-pi-ia šu-kun [kap-pi-ka]
119 ina UGU i-di-ia šu-kun [i-di-ka]
120 ina UGU GABA-šu iš-ta-kan [GABA-su]
121 ina UGU na-aṣ kap-pi-šu iš-ta-kan k[ap-pi-šu]
122 ina UGU i-di-šu iš-ta-kan i-d[i-šu]
123 ú-dan-nin-ma ir-ta-kás bi-lat-su :
124 1-en KASKAL.GÍD ú-šá-q[í-šú-m]a
125 Á.MUŠEN a-na šá-šu-ma a-na ^{d}e-ta-na iz-zak-k[ar-š]ú
126 du-gul ib-ri ma-a-tu ki-i i-ba-á[š]-ši
127 ṣu-ub-bi tam-tum i-da-te-šá bit-[r]i
128 ma-a-tum-me-e li-mid-da KUR-a :
129 tam-tum i-tu-ra a-na me-e-⸢me⸣-e-ma
130 2-a KASKAL.GÍD ú-šá-q[í]-šú-ma
131 Á.MUŠEN a-na šá-šu-ma a-na ^{d}e-ta-na iz-z[ak]-kar
132 du-gul ib-ri ma-a-tum ki-i i-ba-áš-ši :
133 ma-a-tum me-e-me-[e]-ma
134 šal-šá KASKAL.GÍD ú-šá-qí-šú-ma :
135 Á.MUŠEN a-na šá-šu-ma a-na ^{d}e-ta-na iz-[zak-ka]r
136 du-gul ib-ri ma-a-tu ki-i i-ba-[áš-š]i
137 tam-tum i-tu-ra a-na i-ki šá LÚ.NU.GIŠ.[SAR]
138 iš-tu e-lu-ú a-na AN-e šá ^{d}⸢a⸣-[nim]
139 ina KÁ ^{d}a-nim $^{d+}$EN.LÍL u ^{d}É.A i-ba-ʾu-[ú]
140 Á.MUŠEN ^{d}⸢e⸣-[ta-na it-t]i a-ḫa-meš uš-[ke-nu]
141 ina KÁ ^{d}3[0 ^{d}UTU ^{d}IM u ^{d}IŠ.TAR KI.MIN :]
142 [Á.MU]ŠEN ^{d}e-ta-n[a it-ti KI.MIN]
143 e-mur [É ap-ti la-aš-šu NA$_4$.KIŠIB :]
144 [GIŠ.IG-sa i]s-sa-kip-⸢ma⸣ [i-tar-ba-šu]
break of approximately 13 lines
159 [x x x x x x x x x x x x]-kiš

---

160 [x x x x x x x x x x x]-⸢ṣa$^{?}$⸣-ar
161 [DUB 3.KÁM URU i-ṣi-ru ul-tak$^{?}$-li$^{?}$-lu$^{?}$]-šú
162 [É.GAL ^{m}AN.ŠÁR—DÙ—DUMU.UŠ LUGAL ŠÚ LUGAL KUR—AN.ŠÁR.K]I
163 [ša ^{d}AG ^{d}taš-me-tum uz-nu ra-pa-áš-tum] iš-[ru-ku-u]š
164 [i-ḫu-zu IGI.2 na-mir-tum ni-siq] ṭup-š[ar-ru-t]i
165 [ša ina LUGAL.MEŠ a-lik maḫ-ri-ia mám-ma šip-ru šu-a-t]u la ⸢i⸣-[ḫu-z]u
166 [né-me-eq ^{d}AG ti-kip sa-an-tak-k]i ma-la b[a-áš-m]u
167 [ina ṭup-pa-a-ni áš-ṭur as-niq] ab-re-⸢e⸣-[m]a
168 [a-na ta-mar-ti ši-ta-si-ia qé-r]eb É.GAL-ia ⸢ú⸣-[ki]n

mar-ḫi-is-su 88 Cf. line 133 102-107 Cf. lines 139-144 105 Restored from line 140 106 Restoration SP 110 [...]-⸢tar⸣ L 112 at-be-ma a-na-ku K : at-bi-ma ana-ku M 114 ana K : a-na M 115 ib-ri M : [ib]-DIR K 123 or read as ir-ta-bi 133 ma-a-tum⸣ M : -⸢tú⸣ N; cf. line 88 141 Restored from line 104 143f Restored from lines 106f

K 14788

beginning broken away

1 ⸢URU⸣.KI KIŠ.KI *i-ba[k-ki x x x x x x x x x]*
2 *i-na li-ib-bi-šu x[x x x x x x x x x x]*
3 *az-mu-ur x[x x x x x x x x x x]*
4 KIŠ.KI *qa-x[x x x x x x x x x x]*
5 ^{d}*e-ta-na [x x x x x x x x x]*
6 [KIŠ].KI *q[a-x x x x x x x x x x]*
7 *[e-n]u-ma x[x x x x x x x x x x]*
8 [^{d}*e*]*-ta-na [x x x x x x x x x]*
9 *[x x]* ⸢*x x*⸣ *[x x x x x x x x x]*

rest broken away

SCORE

TABLET I

1 A URU *i-ṣi-r[u …]*

2 A [...]*-du-ú* DINGIR.MEŠ […]

3 A [… K]I *ṣi-(ru)* ⸢*i*⸣*-ṣi-ru* ⸢*ul*⸣-[…]

4 A […*-š*]*i-šú id-du-ú* DINGIR.MEŠ […]

5 A ⸢^{d}5⸣.1.1 *ú-kin-nu lib-na-a[s- …]*

6 A [LUGA]L *lu-u re-é-um-ši-n[a …]*

7 A *[e-t]a-na lu-u i-*⸢*tin*⸣*-ši-na e-[…]*

8 A *ši-bir-r[u …]*

9 A *[r]a-bu-tum* ^{d}*a-nun-na-k[i …]*

OB$_{M}$ *ra-bu-tum* ^{d}A.NUN.NA *ša-i-mu ši-im-tim*

10 A *[uš-b]u im-tal-li-ku mi-lik-šú-nu* […]

OB$_{M}$ *uš-bu im-li-ku mi-li-ik-ša ma-a-ta-am*

11 A [...]*-ú kib-ra-a-ti šá-*IM-[…]

OB$_{M}$ *ba-nu ki-ib-ra-tim ša-ki-nu ši-ki-it-tim*

12 A *z[i]-*⸢*ik*⸣*-ri* DÙ*-šú-nu* ^{d}5.⸢1.1⸣ [...] ⸢UN$^{?}$⸣-[…]

OB$_{M}$ *zí-ru a-na ni-ši i-lu i-gi$_{4}$-gu i-sí-nam a-na ni-ši i-ši-mu*

13 A *l[a] iš-ku-nu* [LU]GA[L]

OB$_{M}$ *šar-ra-am la iš-ku-nu ka-lu ni-ši e-pí-a-tim*

14 A *i-na* UD*-mi-šu-ma* […]

OB$_{M}$ *i-na ši-wa-tim la ka-aṣ-ra-at ku-ub-šum me-a-nu*

15 A *ù* GIŠ.PA NA$_{4}$.ZA.GÌN […]

OB$_{M}$ *ù ha-aṭ-ṭù-um uq-ni-a-am la ṣa-ap-ra-at*

16 A *la ba-na-a kib-ra-a-ti* 1*-niš* […]

OB$_{M}$ *la ba-nu-ú iš-ti-ni-iš pa-ra-ak-ku*

17 A ^{d}*se-bet-tum* UGU *um-ma-ni ú-di-*⸢*lu*⸣ […]

OB$_{M}$ *se-bi-ta ba-bu ud-du-lu e-lu da-ap-nim*

18 A UGU *da-ád-me ú-di-lu* […]

19 A URU ^{d}5.1.1 *šu-tas-hu-ru* […]

20 A ^{d}IŠ.TAR *re-é-a* […]

21 A *ù* LUGAL *i-še-*⸢*ʾi*⸣*-i* […]

22 A ^{d}*in-nin-na re-*⸢*é*⸣-[…]

23 A *ù* LUGAL *i-še-*[…]

24 A $^{d+}$EN.LÍL *i-ha-aṭ pa-rak-ki* AN-⸢*e*⸣ […]

25 A *iš-te-né-ʾe-e-ma x*[…]

26 A *ina ma-a-ti* LUGAL […]

27 A LUGAL*-ú-tu* […]

OB$_{M}$ *[šar-r]u-tum i-na ša-ma-i ur-da-am*

28 A *ub-lam-ma* […]

29 A DINGIR.MEŠ KUR-[…]

30 A *[x]x šu x*[…]

57 K [*x x*] *nu x*[…]
58 K [*mar*]*-hi-is-su ana šá-šu-m*[*a* …]
59 K [*šu-u*]*t-tu ia-a-ši ú-*⸢*šab*⸣-[…]
60 K GIM *e-ta-ni mu-ti* ⸢*ku*$^{?}$⸣ *x*[…]
61 K GIM *ka-a-ši* […]
62 K ⸢^{d}⸣*e-ta-na šar-*⸢*ru*⸣ *x*[…]
63 K *e-ṭém-mu-šu ana* [*x*]*x* […]
64 K *ù la* ⸢*ud*$^{?}$⸣ [*x*] ⸢*ina*$^{?}$ É$^{?}$ *x x x*⸣ *x*[…]
65 K *zu x*[...]*x ma x*[…]
66 K ⸢UGU *mu-ut*⸣ [...] ⸢*x x*⸣ […]

TABLET II

1	B$_1$	[*x*]*x-da a-me-lu* MU-*šú i-n*[*am*$^?$-...]
2	B$_1$	[*di*$^?$]-*in-ta i-te-pu-uš* [...]
3	B$_1$	[*p*]*a-rak-ki šá* ^{d}IM DINGIR-*šu* [...]
4	B$_1$	⸢*ina*⸣ GIŠ.MI *pa-rak-ki šá-a-šú a-ṣa-at ṣa*[*r-*...]
5	B$_1$	⸢*ina*⸣ *ap-pi-šá ra-bi-iṣ* Á.MUŠEN [...]
	MA$_1$	*i-na ap-pi* GIŠ Á.MUŠEN *a-li-id-ma i-na eš-di ṣar-bat-te* MUŠ *i-tal-da*
6	B$_1$	⸢UD⸣-*mi-šam-ma i-na-ṣ*[*a-*...]
7	B$_1$	⸢Á⸣.MU[ŠEN ...]
	B$_3$	[... MU]ŠEN KA-*šu i-pu-šam-m*[*a* ...]
8	B$_3$	[*al*]-*ka* ⸢*ni-nu-u-ma ru-u*$_8$*-a*⸣-[...]
9	B$_3$	⸢*lu-u*⸣ *it-ba-ru a-n*[*a-*...]
10	B$_3$	[MUŠ] KA-*šu i-pu-šam-ma* [...]
11	B$_3$	[... *š*]*u-*⸢*u*$^?$⸣ *šá ru-u*$_8$*-a-u-tu x*[...]
12	B$_3$	*l*[*em*$^?$*-né-t*]*a-ma kab-t*[*a-*...]
13	B$_3$	*an-z*[*il-la*] *šá* DINGIR.MEŠ [...]
14	B$_3$	*al-*⸢*ka*⸣ *ni-zaq-pa-am-ma* [...]
15	B$_3$	*ni-it-ma-a* KI-*tim* [...]
16	B$_3$	*ina ma-har* ^{d}UTU *qu-ra-di ma-mit it-*[...]
17	B$_3$	[*šá*] *i-ta-a šá* ^{d}UTU [...]
18	B$_3$	^{d}UTU *lem-niš ina qa-at ma-hi-ṣ*[*i* ...]
	MA$_1$	^{d}*šá-maš lem-na ana* ŠU *ma-hi-ṣi lu-me-li*
19	B$_3$	*šá i-ta-a šá* ^{d}UTU [...]
20	B$_3$	*li-is-su-šu-ma né-re-*[...]
	OB$_S$	*li-ik-la-šu ne-re-eb-ta-šu šà-du-ú*
	MA$_1$	[... *l*]*i-né-a-šu*
21	B$_3$	GIŠ.TUKUL *mur-tap-pi-du* UGU-*šú* [...]
	OB$_S$	*ka-ak-ku-um mu-úr-ta-ap-pi-du e-li-šu li-še-er*
	MA$_1$	[GIŠ.TUKU]L *mul-*⸢*tar-pi*⸣*-du* UGU-*šu li-šir*
22	B$_3$	*giš-par-ru ma-mit* ^{d}UTU *lib-bal-ki-tu-šu-ma l*[*i*$^?$-...]
	MA$_1$	[... *l*]*i-bal-ki-su-m*[*a*] [...] ⸢*e-ta*⸣*-t*[*i-qu*]
23	B$_3$	*iš-tu ma-mit it-mu-ú* KI-*t*[*im* ...]
	OB$_S$	*ma-mi-ta-am ut-ta-ma-am-mu-ú*
24	B$_3$	*iz-zaq-pu-nim-ma šá-da-a e-lu-*⸢*ú*⸣
25	B$_3$	UD-1-KÁM-TA.ÀM *i-na-ṣa-ru* MÁ[Š.ANŠE]
26	B$_3$	GUD.AM *sír-ri-mu* Á.MUŠEN *i-bar-ra*[*m-ma*]
	OB$_S$	*ri-ma šà-ap-pa-ra* MUŠ *i-ba-ra-am-ma*
	MA$_1$	MUŠ *it-ta-ṣi i-ba-ar*
27	B$_3$	MUŠ *ik-kal i-né-e*$^{\flat}$*-ú ik-ka-lu* DUMU.MEŠ-[*šú*]
	MA$_1$	Á.MUŠEN *e-kal i-né-e e-ka-lu* DUMU.MEŠ-*šu*
28	B$_3$	*ar-mi* MAŠ.DÀ.MEŠ MUŠ *i-bar-ram-*[*ma*]

MA_1 *ar-mi* MAŠ.DÀ.MEŠ *ša* EDIN KI.MIN

29 B_3 Á.MUŠEN *ik-kal i-né-e'-ú ik-ka-lu* DUMU.MEŠ-[*šú*]

OB_S *e-ru-ú i-ku-ul i-ku-lu ma-ru-šu*

MA_1 [Á.MUŠE]N *e-kal i-né-e KI*.MIN

30 B_3 *sa-ap-pa-ri di-da-ni* Á.MUŠEN *i-bar-ram-m*[*a*]

31 B_3 [M]UŠ *ik-kal i-né-e'-ú ik-ka-lu* DUMU.MEŠ-[*šú*]

32 B_3 [MÁ]Š?.AN[ŠE? ...]-*ti qaq-qa-ri* MUŠ *i-bar-ram-m*[*a*]

OB_S [...] EDIN *na-maš-ti* KI KI.MIN

33 B_3 [...]-⸢*né-e*'⸣-*ú ik-ka-lu* DUMU.MEŠ-⸢*šú*⸣

MA_1 [...] *e-kal i-né-i* KI.MIN

34 B_2 ⸢DUMU?.MEŠ?⸣ [...]

B_3 [...] ⸢*ú*⸣-*kul-ta* :

35 B_3 ⸢DUMU.MEŠ⸣ Á.MUŠEN *ir-bu-u i-ši-hu*

36 B_2 *iš-tu* DUMU.MEŠ Á.MUŠEN⸣ [...]

B_3 [...] *ir-bu-ú i-ši-hu*

OB_S [*i*]*š-tu ma-ru-šu ir-bu-ú* [...]

MA_1 [... DUMU].MEŠ Á.MUŠEN [*ir-bu*]-⸢*ú*⸣ *i-šu-hu*

37 B_2 Á.MUŠEN ŠÀ-*ba-šu le*-[...]

B_3 [...]-*mut-tu ik-pu-du-m*[*a*]

OB_S ⸢*e*⸣-[*ru-ú i-n*]*a li-ib-bi-šu* [...]

38 B_2 *ik-pu-ud-ma* ŠÀ-*b*[*a*-...]

B_3 [...-*b*]*a-šu le-mut-tu*

39 B_2 *a-na at-mi šá ru-*u_8*-a-šú a-ka-li* [...]

B_3 [...] *p*[*a*?-*ni*?]-*šú iš-kun*

40 B_2 Á.MUŠEN KA-*šu i-pu-uš-ma i-zak-kar* ⸢*a*⸣-[...]

41 B_2 DUMU.MEŠ MUŠ-*mi lu-ku-lu ana-ku* :

OB_S ⸢*ù*⸣ *ma-ru* MUŠ *lu-ku*-[*ul* ...]

42 B_2 MUŠ-*mi* ⸢ŠÀ⸣-[...]

43 B_2 *e-li-ma i-na šá-ma-mi uš*-[*šab*]

OB_S *e-te-el-li-ma i-n*[*a* ...]

44 B_2 *ur-rad i-na ap-pi iṣ-ṣi-ma a-kal* ⸢*in-ba*⸣

F [...]-⸢*na*⸣ *ap*-[...]

OB_S *uš-šà-am-ma* [...]

45 B_2 *at-mu ṣe-eh-ru a-tar ha-si-sa* :

F [... -*e*]*h-ru a-tar* [...]

OB_S *at-mu-u*[*m* ...]

46 B_2 *a-na* Á.MUŠEN AD-*šú* INIM M[U]-⸢*ár*⸣

OB_S *a-na e*-[*ri-i* ...]

47 B_2 *la ta-kal a-bi še-e-tu šá* ^{d}UTU *i-ba-á*[*r-ka*]

F [...] *a-bi še*-⸢*e*⸣-[...]

OB_S [*l*]*a t*[*a-ka-al* ...]

48 B_2 *giš-par-ru ma-mit* ^{d}UTU *ib-bal-ki-tu-ka-ma i-bar-ru*-⸢*nik*⸣-*k*[*a*]

F [... *m*]*a-mit* ^{d}UTU *ib-bal-ki*-⸢*tu*⸣-*k*[*a*-...]

49 B_2 *šá i-ta-a šá* ^{d}UTU *it-ti-qu* :

F [...] *šá* ^{d}UTU *it-ti-qu* :

50	B_2	^{d}UTU *lem-niš ina qa-at* [...]
	F	^{d}UTU [...]
51	B_2	*ul iš-me-šu-nu-ti-ma ul iš-ma-a* [... DU]MU.M[EŠ-*šú*]
	F	[...-*š*]*u-nu-ti-ma* : *ul iš-ma-*[...]
52	B_2	⸢*ú*⸣*-ri-dam-ma e-ta-kal* DUMU.[...]
	F	[...-*da*]*m-ma e-ta-kal* DUMU.[...]
	OB_S	[*m*]*a-ru* MU[Š ...]
53	B_2	⸢*ina*$^{?}$ *li*$^{?}$*-la*$^{?}$⸣*-a-ti ina qer-bit* UD-*me* :
	F	[...]-⸢*a*$^{?}$⸣*-ti ina qer-bit* UD-*me* :
	OB_S	*li-la-tu* [...]
54	B_2	MUŠ [...] U[ZU *i-n*]*a-ši bi-lat-su* :
	F	MUŠ *il-*[... -*n*]*a-ši bi-lat-su* :
	OB_S	MUŠ *i-ku-šà* [...] *ši-i-ra š*[*à* ...] MUŠ *it-ta-di*
55	B_2	*ina* K[Á ...]
	F	*i-na* KÁ *qin-ni-*[*šu* ...]
	OB_S	*ma-ha-ar* [...]
56	B_2	[...]-*ma qin-na-*[...]
	F	[...]-⸢*sa*⸣*-ma qin-na-šú la-áš-šú* :
	OB_S	*ip-pa-li-is-ma la-aš-šu-ú* [...]
57	F	*ú-ši-ir-ma ul* [...]
58	B_2	[...]-*ra-n*[*u-*...]
	F	[...-*r*]*a-nu-uš-šú qaq-qa-ra* [...]
	OB_S	*ṣú-up-ra-nu-uš-šu qa-qa-ra-a*[*m* ...]
59	B_2	[...]-*nu tu*[*r-*...]
	F	*e-l*[*e-n*]*u tur-bu-uʾ-ta-šú šá-ma-m*[*i* ...]
	OB_S	⸢*ù*$^{?}$ *e*$^{?}$*-le*$^{?}$⸣*-num šà-ma-a-a x*[...]
60	F	MUŠ *i-*⸢*na-ʾi*$^{?}$*-il*⸣*-ma i-bak-ki* :
	OB_S	[... *m*]*a-ru-úṣ i-ba-*⸢*ak*⸣-[*ki*]
61	F	*a-na pa-an* ^{d}UTU *i*[*l-*...]
	OB_S	[...] *il-la-ka di-*[*ma-a*]*-šu*
62	F	*at-kal-kúm-ma* ^{d}UTU [...]
	OB_S	*at-*⸢*ka*⸣*-la-ak-ku-um-ma* ^{d}UTU *qú-ra-d*[*u*]
63	F	*a-na* Á.MUŠEN Z[ÍD$^{?}$-...] ⸢*a-na*⸣*-k*[*u* ...]
	OB_S	*a-na e-ri-i* ⸢*im*⸣*-ma-ni a-na-ku aš-ru-k*[*ám*]
64	F	*e-nen-na qin-ni* [...]
65	F	*qin-ni ia-ú la-áš-*[*š*]*u* ⸢*qin*⸣-[...]
	OB_S	*šu-ú qí-in-na-šu šà-li-im-ma sà-pi-ih qí-in-*[*ni*]
66	F	*sa-ap-hu at-mu-ú-a ša*[*l-*...]
	OB_S	*šà-al-mu at-mu-šu la-aš-šu-ú ma-ru-ú-a*
67	F	*ú-ri-dam-ma e-ta-kal* [...]
	OB_S	*úr-da-am-ma i-ta-ka-al li-da-ni-ia*
68	F	⸢*lum*⸣*-nu šá i-pu-šá-an-ni* ^{d}U[TU ...]
	OB_S	*lum-na il-li-ka* ^{d}UTU *lu ti-de*
69	F	*a-bar-šá* ^{d}UTU *še-et-ka er-ṣe-*[...]
	OB_S	*še-et-ka qé-er-bé-tu ra-pa-*[*aš-tum*]
70	F	*giš-par-ru-ka* AN-*ú* [...]

OB$_S$ gi-iš-pe-er-ra-ka [… ru-qú]-tu
71 F i-na še-ti-ka a-a ú-ṣ[i …]
OB$_S$ i-na še-ti-ka a-a [...] e-ru-ú
72 F e-piš HUL-tim an-zu-ú mu-˹kil˺ […]
OB$_S$ e-pi-iš le-mu-[ut-ti ù a]n-zi-il-li mu-ki-il le-m[u-ut-t]i a-na ib-ri-šu
73 F un-né-ni šá MUŠ […]
74 F ^{d}UTU KA-šu i-pu-šá-˹am˺-ma a-n[a …]
75 F a-lik ur-ha e-ti-i[q …]
76 F ˹uk˺-ta-as-si-ka ri-[mu]
77 F [pe]-˹te-e˺-ma ŠÀ-ba-šu […]
78 F ˹šu-ub˺-ta id-di […]
79 F [...] iṣ-˹ṣu-rat˺ šá-ma-me […]
80 F [Á.MU]ŠEN it-ti-˹ši˺-n[a …]
81 F [ki$^{?}$] ˹la˺ i-du-ú-[…]
G […-m]a ˹a˺-n[a$^{?}$ …]
82 F nu-ru-ub UZU iš-te-né-[…]
G [...]-˹ub UZU˺ iš-te-˹né-e᾽-i˺ sa-˹da˺-a-ti it-ta-na-al-˹lak˺
83 F a-na ku-tu-um Š[À-…]
G a-na ku-tu-um ŠÀ-bi uš-ta-ma-˹aṣ-ṣa˺
84 F a-na ŠÀ-bi ˹ina e˺-re-˹bi˺-š[u :] ˹at-[…]
G a-na ŠÀ-bi i-na e-re-˹bi-šu˺ at-ta ṣa-bat-su i-n[a] ˹kap-pi˺-šú
85 F nu-˹uk˺-kis kap-pi-šu ab-ri-[…]
G nu-uk-kis kap-pi-šú ab-ri-šú ù n[u-bal-l]i-šú
86 F bu-qu-un-šu-ma i-di-šú ana ˹šu-ut-t[a-…]
G bu-qu-un-šú-ma id-di ana šu-ut-ta-ti ˹ša la ^{d}UTU˺-ši
87 F mu-ut bu-bu-ti ù ṣu-um-[…]
G mu-ut bu-bu-ti ù ṣu-mi ˹li-mu-ta˺
88 F a-na zi-kir ^{d}UTU qu-ra-di :
G a-na zi-kir ^{d}UTU qu-˹ra-du˺
89 F MUŠ i[l-…]
G MUŠ il-lik i-ti-iq šá-˹da˺-a
90 F ik-šu-ud-ma MUŠ a-[…]
G ik-šu-ud-ma MUŠ a-na ṣe-e[r ri]-mi
91 F ip-te-e-ma ŠÀ-ba-šú k[a-…]
G ip-te-e-ma ŠÀ-ba-šú ka-ra-˹as˺-s[u iš]-˹ṭu˺-uṭ
92 F šu-ub-ta id-di […]
G šu-ub-ta it-ta-di i-na kar-ši-šú
93 F mim-mu-ú iṣ-ṣu-rat šá-ma-me ˹ú˺-[…]
G mim-mu-ú iṣ-ṣu-rat šá-ma-mi [...]-˹da˺-ma ik-ka-la ši-i-ra
94 B$_2$ [...] ˹lu$^{?}$˺-[m]u$^{?}$-u[n$^{?}$-…]
F Á.MUŠEN lu-mu-u[n-…]
G [Á.MU]ŠEN lu-mu-un-šú i-[d]a-a-ma
95 B$_2$ [...] iṣ-ṣu-ri […]
F it-ti DUMU.MEŠ iṣ-ṣ[u-…]
G [it-t]i DUMU.MEŠ iṣ-ṣ[u-r]i ul ik-kal ši-i-ra
96 B$_2$ [Á.MU]ŠEN ˹KA˺-šu i-pu-šá-am-ma i-[…]

	F	⸢Á⸣.MUŠEN *pa-a-šu i-pu-š[á-…]*
	G	*[...] i-pu-šam-ma i-zak-ka-ra ana* DUMU.MEŠ-*šú*
97	B_2	*[al-k]a-[…]*
	F	*[al]-ka-nim-ma i ni-rid-[…]*
	G	*[… n]i-rid-ma* UZU AM *an-né-e i ni-ku-la ni-nu*
98	B_2	*[at]-mu ṣ[e-eh]-ru a-[tar h]a-[si-sa :]*
	F	*[at]-mu ṣe-eh-ru a-[…]*
	G	*[...]-⸢eh⸣-ru a-tar ha-si-sa*
	MA_1	AMAR TUR *a-tar h[a-…]*
99	G	*[...]-ma-tum i-zak-kar*
	MA_1	*ana* Á.MUŠEN *a-bi-šu […]*
100	B_2	*[la t]ur-r[ad] a-⸢bi mìn-de ina* ŠÀ-*bi* AM⸣ *a[n-...]* ⸢MUŠ⸣ […]
	F	*[...]-rad a-bi mìn-de […]*
	G	[… A]M *an-né-e* MUŠ *ra-bi-iṣ*
	MA_1	*la tu-rad mìn-d[e …]*
101	B_2	⸢Á⸣.MUŠEN ⸢*it*⸣*-ti* ⸢ŠÀ?-*bi*?-*šú a*⸣*-ma-tu i-qa[b-bi]*
	F	*[...] it-ti [… ...]-ma-[…]*
	G	*[…-m]a-tum i-qab-bi*
102	B_2	*[iṣ-ṣ]u-⸢ra-a-tu⸣ [...]-⸢ti?⸣ ki-i-mi ik-ka-la š[i-ra?]*
	F	*[…-r]a-a-t[u ...]-ti [… i]k-ka-la […]*
103	B_2	*[u]l iš-me-[šú]-nu-ti-ma ⸢ul⸣ iš-ma-a zi-kir* DUM[U.MEŠ]-*šú*
	F	*[…-t]i-ma ul iš-ma-[…]*
	MA_1	*ul i-še[m-me …]*
104	B_2	*ú-⸢ri-dam⸣-ma it-ta-ziz ina* UGU *ri-me*
	F	*[…-t]a-ziz ina* UGU *ri-mi* :
	MA_1	*ur-da-m[a …]*
105	B_2	Á.MUŠEN ⸢*ip-ta*⸣*-qid* UZU :
	F	⸢Á⸣.[…]
106	B_2	*iš-te-né-e᾿-i šá pa-ni-šú ù ⸢ár⸣-[k]i-šú*
	F	*[...]-i šá pa-ni-šú […]*
	MA_1	1.TA [...] Á.MUŠEN *ip-[...] mar-[…]*
107	B_2	*iš-ni-i᾿ ip-⸢ta⸣-qid* UZU
	F	*[… i]p-ta-qid* UZU :
	MA_1	*iš-ni i[š-…]* Á.MUŠEN *ip-pa-[…]*
108	B_2	*iš-te-né-e᾿-i šá pa-ni-šú ù ⸢ár⸣-[k]i-šú*
	F	*i[š]-te-n[é-…]*
	MA_1	*ú-še-liš i[š-…]* Á.MUŠEN *ip-pa-[…]*
109	B_2	*sa-da-a-⸢ti⸣ [it]-ta-na-al-lak*
	F	*[…-a]l-lak* :
110	B_2	*a-na ku-⸢tùm⸣* ŠÀ-*bi uš-ta-ma-⸢aṣ⸣-ṣa*
	F	*a-n[a …]*
	MA_1	*a-na ka-ra-áš* A[M …]
111	B_2	*a-na* Š[À-*b*]*i ina e-re-bi-šú* :

	F	[...-*r*]*e*-⸢*bi*⸣-*šu* :
	MA_1	*a-na qer-bu-uš* ⸢*i*⸣-[*na* ...]
112	B_2	MUŠ *iṣ-ṣa-bat-su ina kap-pi-šú*
	MA_1	MUŠ *iṣ-ṣa-ba-su* [...]
113	B_2	TU-*ub* KU-NE-*en-ni* TU-*ub* KU-NE-*en-ni*
	F	[...-N]E-*en-ni* [...]
114	B_2	Á.MUŠEN K[A-*šu*] ⸢*i-pu*⸣-*šá-am-ma a-na* MUŠ *i-zak-kar-šú*
	F	[...] ⸢*i*⸣-*pu-šá-a*[*m*]-⸢*ma*⸣ [...]
115	B_2	⸢ARHUŠ⸣-*an-ni-ma* GIM *e-re-ši nu-dun-na-a lud-din*-⸢*ka*⸣
	F	[...] GIM *e-re*-⸢*ši*⸣ *n*[*u*-...]
116	B_2	MUŠ KA-*šu i-pu-šá-am-ma a-na* Á.MUŠEN *i-zak*-⸢*kar*⸣-*šú*
	F	[...-*p*]*u-šá-am-ma* ⸢*a*⸣-*na* ⸢Á⸣.[...]
	OB_M	*ṣe-ru p*[*a*-...]
117	B_2	*ú-maš-šar-ka-ma* ^{d}UTU *e-le-nu ki-i ap*-⸢*pal*⸣
	F	[...-*m*]*a* ^{d}UTU ⸢*e*⸣-*l*[*e*-...]
	OB_M	*ma-a ú-wa*-[*aš-šar* ...]
118	B_2	*še-ret-ka i-sah-hu-ra a-na* UGU-*hi-ia*
	F	[...] *i-s*[*ah*]-*hu*-[...]
	OB_M	*ši-ri-it-k*[*a* ...]
119	B_2	*šá a-šak-ka-nu-ka a-na-ku še-er-ta*
	F	[...-*k*]*a a-n*[*a*-...]
120	B_2	*ú-nak-ki-is kap-pi-šú ab-ri-šú nu-bal-li-šú*
	OB_M	*ut-ta-zí*-[*ik* ...]
121	B_2	[...-*u*]*n-šu-ma id*-[...]
	B_3	[...] ⸢*šu-ut*⸣-[...]
	OB_M	*ib-qú-un-šu-m*[*a* ...]
122	B_2	[...] *bu-bu-t*[*i* ...]
	B_3	[...]-*i i-m*[*a-at*]
123	B_3	[Á.MUŠEN$^{?}$ ...]-⸢*ti*⸣ [...-*m*]*a*
124	B_3	⸢UD⸣-*mì-šam-ma im-da-na-ha-ra* ⸢^{d}UTU⸣
	OB_M	UD-*mi-ša-am-ma* [...]
125	B_3	[...]-*na šu-ut-ta-ti a-ma-ta-ma* :
126	B_3	*man-nu i-di ki-i šak-na-ku še-ret-ka*
127	B_3	[*i*]*a-a-ši* Á.MUŠEN *bul-liṭ-an-ni-ma*
	OB_M	*ia-ti-i*-[*ma* ...]
128	B_3	[*a-n*]*a* UD-*mi da-ru-ú-ti zi-kir-ka lu-uš-te-eš-me*
129	B_3	^{d}UTU KA-*šú* DÙ-*uš-ma a-na* Á.MUŠEN *i-zak-kar-š*[*ú*]
	G	[...]-*šú*
	OB_M	^{d}UTU *pi-šu i-p*[*u*-...]
130	B_3	*lem-né-ta-ma kab-ta-ti tu-šam-ri-i*[*ṣ*]
	G	[...]-*iṣ*
	OB_M	*le-em-né-ti k*[*ab*-...]
131	B_3	*an-zil-la šá* DINGIR.MEŠ *a-sak-ku ta-ku*[*l*]

	G	[*...-k*]*u*-⸢*ul*⸣
	OB$_M$	*an-zi-lam ša i*-[*li* ...]
132	B$_3$	*ta-ma-ta-a-ma la a-sa-an-ni-qa-ak-ka*
	G	*t*[*a*-...]-*ka*
133	B$_3$	*a-lik a-me-la šá a-šap-pa-rak-ka* ŠU-*ka li-iṣ-bat*
	G	*a-l*[*i*-... *li-i*]*ṣ-bat*
134	B$_3$	^{d}*e-ta-na* UD-*mì-šam-ma im-ta-ah-ha-ra* ^{d}UTU
	G	^{d}*e-t*[*a*-...]-*ši*
135	B$_3$	*ta-kul* ^{d}UTU *ku-bur šu-u*ʾ*-e-a* :
	G	*ta-kul* ⸢^{d}⸣[...]-⸢*e*⸣-*a*
136	B$_3$	KI-*tum taš-ti-i da-am as-li*-[*ia*]
	G	*er-ṣe-t*[*um* ...]-⸢*li*⸣-*ia*
137	B$_3$	DINGIR.MEŠ *ú-kab-bit e-ṭém-me ap-là*[*h*]
	G	DINGIR.MEŠ ⸢*ú*⸣-[...]-*làh*
138	B$_3$	*ig-dam-ra maš-šak-ki-ia* MÍ.EN.ME.LI.ME[Š]
	G	*ig-dam-ra* ⸢*maš-šak-ki*⸣-[... L]I.MEŠ
139	B$_3$	*as-li-ia ina ṭu-ub-bu-hi* DINGIR.MEŠ *ig-dam-r*[*u*]
	G	*as-li-ia i-na ṭu-ub*-⸢*bu-hi*⸣ DINGIR.MEŠ *ig-dam-ru*
140	B$_3$	*be-lum ina pi-i-ka li-ṣa-am-ma* :
	G	*be-lí i-na pi-i-ka li-ṣa-am-ma*
141	B$_3$	*id-nam-ma šam-ma šá a-l*[*a-di*]
	G	*id-nam-ma šam-ma šá a-la-di*
	MA$_4$	[... *š*]*a*-⸢*la-di šam-ma*⸣ [... *ia*]-*ti*
142	B$_3$	*kul-li-man-ni-ma šam-ma šá a-la-di* :
	G	*kul-li-man-ni-ma šam-ma šá a-la-di*
143	B$_3$	*pil-ti ú-suh-ma šu*-[...]
	G	*pil-ti ú-suh-ma šu-ma šuk-na-an-ni*
	MA$_4$	[*pí*]*l-ti ú-suh$_4$-ma šu-ma šuk-na-ni*
144	B$_3$	^{d}UTU KA-*šu i-pu-uš-ma a-na* ^{d}*e-ta-na i-zak*-[...]
	G	^{d}UTU *pi-i-šu i-pu*-⸢*šam-ma*⸣ *a-na* ^{m}*e-ta-na i-zak-kar-šú*
145	B$_3$	*a-lik ur-ha e-ti-iq* KUR-*a* :
	G	[*a-l*]*ik ur-ha* ⸢*e*⸣-*ti-iq šá-da-a*
	MA$_4$	*a-lik* ITI *e-tiq* KUR-*ma*
146	B$_3$	*a-mur šu-ut-ta-tum qé-r*[*eb*-...]
	G	[... *q*]*é-reb-šá bit-ri*
	MA$_4$	[*na-ap-l*]*i-is šu-ta-ta qé-reb-ša qí-it-ru-ub*
147	B$_3$	*i-na* ŠÀ-*bi-šá na-di* Á.MUŠEN :
	G	[...]-⸢*di e*⸣-*ru-ú*
	MA$_4$	*i-na* ŠÀ-*ša* Á.MUŠEN *na-di-ma*
148	B$_3$	*ú-kal-lam-ka šam-m*[*a* ...]
	G	[*...-d*]*i*
	MA$_4$	*šu-ú i-na-di-na-ku ša-la-di šam*-⸢*ma*⸣
149	B$_3$	*a-na zi-kir* ^{d}UTU *qu-ra-di* :
150	B$_3$	^{d}*e-ta-na il-lik* [...]
151	B$_3$	*i-mur-ma šu-ut-ta-tum qé-reb-šá ib-ri* :
152	B$_3$	*ina* ŠÀ-[...]

153	A	*ul-la-nu-um-ma uš-ta-qa-áš-š[ú ...]*
	B_3	*ul-la-nu-um-ma ul-taq-qa-á[š-...]*

154	A	Á.MUŠEN *pi-i-šu i-pu-šam-ma a-na* ^{d}UTU EN-*šú* IN[IM ...]
	B_3	Á.MUŠEN KA-*šu i-pu-šam-ma ana* ^{d}UTU EN-*šú* [...]
155	A	DUB 3.KÁM URU *i-ṣ[i-...]*
	B_3	DUB 2.KÁM URU *i-ṣi-r[u ...]*
156	B_3	É.GAL ^{m}AN.ŠÁR—DÙ—DUMU.UŠ LUGAL ŠÚ [...]
157	B_3	*ša* ^{d}AG ^{d}*taš-me-tum uz-nu ra-p[a-...]*
158	B_3	*i-hu-uz-zu* IGI.2 *na-mir-tum* [...]
159	B_3	*ša ina* LUGAL.MEŠ *a-lik mah-ri-ia mám-*[...]

TABLET III

1	N	[Á].MUŠEN ⸢*pi-i*⸣*-š*[*u* …]
2	N	[*be-l*]*í x*[*x*] *x*[*x* …]
3	N	[*a*]*t-*[*m*]*i iṣ-ṣu-ri* […]
4	N	[…-*r*]*a-ku-ma* […]
5	N	[*mim*]*-mu-ú šu-ú i-qab-b*[*u-*…]
6	N	[*m*]*im-mu-ú a-na-ku a-qab-bu-*[…]
7	N	*ina pi-i* ^{d}UTU *qu-r*[*a-*…]
8	N	*at-mi iṣ-ṣu-ri* […]
9	H	[…-*t*]*a-na i-zak-*⸢*kar-šú*⸣
	N	Á.MUŠEN *pi-i-šu i-pu-š*[*am-*…]
10	H	[...]-⸢*a*⸣*-am at-ta*
	N	[*mi*]*-na-a tal-li-ka* […]
11	H	[...] ⸢Á⸣.MUŠEN *i-zak-kar-šú*
	N	[^{d}]*e-ta-na pi-i-šu i-pu-ša*[*m-*…]
12	H	[… *ša*]*m-ma šá a-la-di*
	N	⸢*ib*⸣*-ri id-nam-*⸢*ma*⸣ […]
13	H	[… *ša*]*m-ma šá a-la-di*
	N	⸢*kul-li-man*⸣*-n*[*i* …]
14	H	[… *š*]*u-ma šuk-na-an-ni*
	N	*pil-ta* […]
15	H	[…-*m*]*a šá a-la-di*
	N	⸢*e*⸣*-zi-ib-ma* […]
16	H	[… *x*]*x a-ṣu-*⸢*ú*⸣
	N	⸢MUŠEN$^{?}$⸣ *ina ṣi-t*[*i*$^{?}$*-*…]
17	H	[…-*a*]*n-ni*
	N	⸢*le*$^{?}$⸣*-qé-a-am* […]
18	H	[...] KUR-*a*
	N	[*e-d*]*in-nu-ia-a-ma l*[*u-*…]
19	H	[...]-⸢*la-di*⸣
	N	[*lu*]*-bi-la-ku-um-ma* […]
20	N	[*i*]*l-lik-ma e-*[…]
21	N	⸢Á⸣.MUŠEN *iṣ-ṣu-da* […]
22	N	*ul i-ba-áš-ši* […]
23	N	*al-ka ib-ri* […]
24	N	*it-ti* ^{d}IŠ.TAR GAŠAN […]
25	N	*ina le-et* ^{d}IŠ.TAR GAŠAN […]
	O	*i*[*na* …]

Line	MS	Text
26	N	ina UGU Á-ia […]
	O	ina […]
27	N	ina UGU na-aṣ kap-pi-i[a …]
	O	ina U[GU …]
28	N	[ina] UGU Á-šu iš-ta-ka[n …]
	O	ina U[GU …]
29	N	[in]a UGU na-aṣ kap-pi-šu […]
	O	ina U[GU …]
30	N	[...] 1.KASKAL.GÍD […]
	O	iš-t[in …]
31	M	[...] ⸢nap-li-is⸣ ma-a-t[um? …]
	N	[ib-r]i nap-lis-ma ma-⸢a-tú⸣ k[i-…]
	O	ib-r[i …]
32	M	[šá] ⸢ma-a⸣-ti i-ha-am-b[u-…]
	N	[šá m]a-a-ti i-ha-a[m-…]
	O	šá ma-a-[…]
33	M	ù tam-tum DAGAL-tum ma-la tar-ba-ṣi :
	N	⸢ù⸣ tam-⸢tu DAGAL-tum⸣ […]
	O	ù tam-t[um …]
34	M	šá-na-a […]
	N	šá-na-a 1 KASKAL.G[ÍD…]
	O	šá-na-a KASKA[L.…]
35	M	ib-ri nap-li-is ma-a-tum ki-i […]
	N	⸢ib⸣-ri nap-li-is-⸢ma ma-a⸣-tu k[i-…]
	O	ib-ri nap-l[i-…]
36	M	⸢it⸣-tur ma-a-tu a-na mu-sa-re-e x[x …]
	N	⸢it⸣-tu-ru ma-⸢a⸣-[tu] a-na[…]
	O	it-tur ma-a-[…]
37	M	ù tam-tum DAGAL-tu ma-la bu-gi-in-ni :
	N	[ù] tam-tu [DAGAL-t]u […]
	O	ù tam-tum DAGA[L-…]
38	M	šal-šá KASK[AL.GÍD u]l-⸢li⸣-šu-ma
	N	[šal]-šá [1.KASKA]L. ⸢GÍD⸣ […]
	O	šal-šá KASKAL.GÍD […]
39	M	ib-ri nap-li-is ma-a-tu ki-i mì-n[i-i] ⸢i⸣-ba-áš-ši
	O	ib-ri nap-li-i[s …]
40	M	ap-pal-sa-am-ma ma-a-tu u[l] a-na-ṭal
	O	ap-pal-sa-a[m-…]
41	M	ù tam-tum DAGAL-tum ul i-šeb-ba-a ⸢i⸣-na-a-a
	O	ù tam-tum DAGA[L-…]
42	M	ib-ri ul e-li a-na AN-e :
	O	ib-ri ul ⸢e⸣-[…]
43	M	šu-kun kib-su lu-ut-[t]al-lak a-na URU-ia
	O	šu-kun kib-[…]
44	M	iš-tin KASKAL.GÍD is-su-ka-áš-šum-ma
45	M	Á.MUŠEN im-qu-ut-ma im-da-har-šu ina kap-pi-šu

46	M	*šá-na-a* KASKAL.GÍD *is-su-ka-áš-šum-ma*
47	M	Á.MUŠEN *im-qu-ut-ma im-da-har-šu* ⸢*ina*⸣ [*kap*]-⸢*pi*⸣-*šu*
48	M	*šal-šá* KASKAL.GÍD ⸢*is*⸣-*s*[*u-...-m*]*a*
49	M	Á.MUŠEN *im-qu-ut-ma im-da-har-*[…]
50	M	[*n*]*ik-kàs a-na qaq-qa-ri* […]
51	M	[Á].MUŠEN *im-qu-ut-ma im-d*[*a-*…]
52	M	[…*-m*]*a* Á.MUŠEN *i-tar-rak* :
53	M	*šá e-t*[*a-na* …]
54	M	[*x x x*]*x x*[*x* …]
55	M	[*x x x*] *lak ka ta* […]
56	M	[...] ⸢*x x*⸣ […]
70	C	[…*-k*]*a-ma* [...] ⸢*dam*⸣ […]
71	C	[...] ⸢*e*⸣-*ta*-⸢*nap-pal*⸣-[*k*]*a*
72	C	[...] ⸢*ú*$^{?}$⸣-*tab-bi-ku-šú* :
73	C	*ik-šud-ma* ⸢URU⸣-*šu u* É-*su*
74	C	[...] *ana* ^{d}⸢*e-ta*⸣-*ni i-zak-kar-šu*
75	C	[...] *šam-mu šá a-la-di*
76	C	[...]*x te-qí-tu*
77	C	[...]-*mu-ra ṣi-is-su*
78	C	[...] *ana* ⸢*ka*⸣-*šá li-ih*-⸢*di*⸣
79	C	[...] *ana* ⸢^{d}⸣*e*-⸢*ta*⸣-*ni i*-[…]
80	C	[...] ⸢*x*⸣ […]
81	C	[...] ⸢*x*⸣ […]
82	C	[...] ⸢*x an*⸣ *šu ki*$^{?}$ *x*[…]
83	C	[...] *ul ib*-[*ši*$^{?}$]
84	C	[… *it*$^{?}$-*t*]*a*$^{?}$-*ṣi* MU.AN.⸢NA$^{?}$⸣
85	C	[...] *ik-šu-dam-ma* […]
86	C	[...]*x pa-ni-šú iš-ku*[*n*]
87	C	[...]-*šú i-pa-šar*
88	C	[… *ma-t*]*um me-e-me-e-ma*
89	C	[...]*x-bi*
90	C	[...]*x-ma*
91	C	[...]*x* ⸢È⸣
92	C	[...]*x*
100	K	⸢$^{d?}$*e*$^{?}$⸣-[...] *pi*-[*i*]-⸢*šú*$^{?}$ DÙ$^{?}$⸣-[…]
101	K	*i*[*b-...-r*]*a-a* DINGIR$^{?}$ ⸢*šu*$^{?}$-*u*$^{?}$-*ma*$^{?}$⸣ […]
102	K	⸢*né-reb šá*⸣ KÁ ^{d}*a-nim* $^{d+}$EN.LÍ[L …]
	L	[...] ⸢^{d}⸣É.[A *n*]*i-ba-ʾu*-⸢*ú*⸣
103	K	*nu-uš-ke-nu* […]
	L	[…*-n*]*a-ku u at-*[*ta*]
104	K	⸢*né-reb šá*⸣ KÁ ^{d}30 ^{d}UTU ^{d}IM *u* ⸢^{d}⸣[…]
	L	[...] *u* ^{d}IŠ.TAR⸣ *ni-ba-ʾu*-⸢*ú*⸣
	M	⸢*né*$^{?}$-*r*[*eb*$^{?}$ …]
105	L	[...] *a-na-ku u at-*[*ta*]
106	K	⸢*a-mur*⸣ É *ap-ti l*[*a-*…]

	L	[...] NA$_4$.KIŠIB [0]
	M	*a-mu*[*r* ...]
107	K	⸢GIŠ.IG⸣-[*s*]*a a-sa-kip*-[...]
	L	[...-*k*]*ip-ma e-tar-ba-áš*-[*šu*]
108	K	⸢*áš-bat*⸣ *ina* ⸢ŠÀ-*bi* 1-*e*[*t*]
	L	[...] 1-*et* [...]
	M	*áš-bat ina* ŠÀ-*bi*⸣ [...]
109	K	⸢AGA⸣ *ru-uṣ-ṣu-na-at* [...]
	L	[...] ⸢DÙ⸣ [M]ÚŠ-[*šá*]
110	K	GIŠ.GU.ZA ŠUB-*ma* DINGIR-*u*-[...]
	L	[... *š*]*u*$^{?}$-*taq-ba*-[...]
	M	GIŠ.GU.ZA ŠU[B-...]
111	K	*ina šap-la* GIŠ.GU.ZA *la-b*[*e* ...]
	L	[... *r*]*ab*-[...]
	M	*ina šap-la* GIŠ.GU.ZA [...]
112	K	⸢*at*⸣-*be-ma a-na-ku la-be i*[*š*-...]
	M	*at-bi-ma ana-ku* [...]
113	K	⸢*ag*⸣-*gal-tam-ma ap-ta-ru-u*[*d* ...]
	M	*ag-gal-tam-ma* [...]
114	K	⸢Á⸣.MUŠEN *ana šá-šu-ma ana* ^{d}*e-ta-na* [...]
	M	Á.MUŠEN *a-na šá-šu-ma a-na* ⸢^{d}*e-ta*⸣-[...]
115	K	[*ib*]-DIR *šu-pa-a* MÁ[Š ...]
	M	*ib-ri šu-pa-a* [...]
116	K	*al-ka lu-uš-ši-ka-ma* [...]
	M	*al-ka lu-uš-ši-ka-ma a-na* AN-*e* [...]
117	K	[*ina*] UGU ⸢GABA-*ia*⸣ [...]
	M	*ina* UGU GABA-*ia šu-kun* [...]
118	M	*ina* UGU *na-aṣ kap-pi-ia šu-kun* [...]
119	M	*ina* UGU *i-di-ia šu-kun* [...]
120	M	*ina* UGU GABA-*šu iš-ta-kan* [...]
121	M	*ina* UGU *na-aṣ kap-pi-šu iš-ta-kan k*[*ap*-...]
122	M	*ina* UGU *i-di-šu iš-ta-kan i-d*[*i-šu*]
123	M	*ú-dan-nin-ma ir-ta-kás bi-lat-su* :
124	M	1-*en* KASKAL.GÍD *ú-šá-q*[*í-šú-m*]*a*
125	M	Á.MUŠEN *a-na šá-šu-ma a-na* ^{d}*e-ta-na iz-zak-k*[*ar-š*]*ú*
126	M	*du-gul ib-ri ma-a-tu ki-i i-ba-á*[*š*]-*ši*
127	M	*ṣu-ub-bi tam-tum i-da-te-šá bit*-[*r*]*i*
128	M	*ma-a-tum-me-e li-mid-da* KUR-*a* :
129	M	*tam-tum i-tu-ra a-na me*-⸢*e-me*⸣-*e-ma*
130	M	2-*a* KASKAL.GÍD *ú-šá-q*[*í*]-⸢*šú*⸣-*ma*
131	M	Á.MUŠEN *a-na šá-šu-ma a-na* ^{d}*e-ta-na iz-z*[*ak*]-*kar*
132	M	*du-gul ib-ri ma-a-tum ki-i i-ba-áš-ši* :
133	M	*ma-a-tum me-e-me*-[*e*$^{?}$]-*ma*
	N	⸢*ma*⸣-*a*-⸢*tú*⸣ [...]
	MA$_3$	[...-*t*]*u i-tu-ra a-n*[*a m*]*e*-⸢*e-me-e*⸣-[*ma*]

134	M	šal-šá KASKAL.GÍD ú-šá-qí-šú-ma :
	N	ša[l-šá 1.KASK]AL.[…]
	MA_3	[ša-al]-šá b[e]-ra u[l]-⌈li⌉-[šu]
135	M	Á.MUŠEN a-na šá-šu-ma a-na [d]e-ta-na iz-[zak-ka]r
	N	⌈Á⌉.MUŠEN […]
	MA_3	[Á.MUŠE]N [a-na šu-a-šu a-na [m]]⌈e⌉-[t]a-na x[...] x[…]
136	M	du-gul ib-ri ma-a-tu ki-i i-b[a-áš-š]i
	N	du-gul […]
	MA_3	[...] ib-ri KUR ⌈ki-i⌉ […]
137	M	tam-tum i-tu-ra a-na i-ki šá LÚ.NU.GI[Š.SAR]
	N	tam-⌈tum i⌉-[…]
	MA_3	[… i]-tu-r[a ki]-i A.MEŠ PA$_5$-ma
138	M	iš-tu e-lu-ú a-na AN-e šá [d]⌈a⌉-[nim]
	N	⌈iš⌉-tu ⌈e⌉-[…]
139	M	[i]na KÁ [d]a-nim [d+]EN.LÍL u [d]É.A i-ba-ʾu-[ú]
	N	ina KÁ [d]⌈a⌉-[…]
140	M	⌈Á⌉.MUŠEN [d]⌈e⌉-[… it-t]i a-ha-meš u[š-…]
	N	⌈Á⌉.MUŠEN [d][…]
141	M	[ina] ⌈KÁ [d]⌉[…]
	N	ina KÁ [d]3[0 …]
142	M	[Á].⌈MUŠEN⌉ [d]e-ta-n[a …]
	N	⌈Á.MUŠEN [d]⌉[…]
143	N	e-mur […]
144	M	[… i]s-sa-⌈kip-ma⌉ […]
159	H	[...]-kiš
160	H	[...]-⌈ṣa[?]⌉-ar
161	H	[...]-šú
162	H	[… AN.ŠÁR.K]I
163	H	[...] iš-[ru-ku-u]š
164	H	[...] ṭup-š[ar-ru-t]i
165	H	[…-t]u la ⌈i⌉-[hu-z]u
166	H	[…-k]i ma-la b[a-áš-m]u
167	H	[...] ab-re-⌈e⌉-[m]a
168	H	[… qé-r]eb É.GAL-ia ⌈ú⌉-[ki]n

GLOSSARY AND INDICES

Logograms and Their Readings

AD → *abu;* AGA → *agû;* AM → *rīmu;* AN → *šamû;* ARHUŠ → *rêmu;* Á → *idu;* Á.MUŠEN → *arû;* d+EN.LÍL → *Illil;* dAG → *Nabû;* dÉ.A → *Ea;* dIM → *Adad;* dIŠ.TAR → *Ištār;* dUTU → *Šamaš, šamšu;* d30 → *Sîn;*
DAGAL → *rapāšu;* DINGIR → *ilu, ilūtu;* DUB → *ṭuppu;* DUMU → *māru;* DÙ → *epēšu, kalu;*
EDIN → *ṣēru;* EN → *bēlu;* É → *bētu;* É.GAL → *ekallu;* È → *aṣû;*
GABA → *irtu;* GAL → *rabû;* GAŠAN → *bēltu;* GIM → *kīma;* GIŠ.GU.ZA → *kussû;* GIŠ.IG → *daltu;* GIŠ.MI → *ṣillu;* GIŠ.PA → *haṭṭu;* GIŠ.TUKUL → *kakku;* GUD.AM → *rīmu;*
HUL → *lemuttu;*
IGI.2 → *īnu;* INIM → *amatu;*
KA → *pû;* KASKAL.GÍD → *bēru;* KÁ → *bābu;* KI → *erṣetu;* KI.SIKIL → *ardatu;* KIŠ.KI → *Kīš;* KUR → *mātu, šadû;* KUR—AN.ŠÁR.KI → *Māt Aššūr;*
LUGAL → *šarru, šarrūtu;* LÚ.NU.GIŠ.SAR → *nukaribbu;*
MAŠ.DÁ → *ṣabītu;* MÁŠ.ANŠE → *būlu;* MÁŠ.MI → *šuttu;* MÍ.EN.ME.LI → *šāʾiltu;* MU → *šumu, zakāru;* MU.AN.NA → *šattu;* MUŠ → *ṣerru;* MUŠEN → *iṣṣūru;* MÚŠ → *zīmu;*
NA_4.KIŠIB → *kunukku;* NA_4.ZA.GÌN → *uqnû;*
ŠÀ → *libbu;* ŠU → *qātu;* ŠUB → *nadû;* ŠÚ → *kiššatu;*
TU → *erēbu;*
UD → *ūmišam, ūmu;* UD.1.KÁM.TA.ÀM → *ūmišamma;* UGU → *muhhu;* UN → *nīšū;* URU → *ālu;* URU.KI → *ālu;* UZU → *šīru;*
ZÍD.$MUNU_4$ → *isimmānu;*
1 → *ištēn, ištēniš, ištēt;* 1.KÁM → *mahrû;* 2 → *šanû B;* 2.KÁM → *šanû B;* 3.KÁM → *šalšu*

Glossary

abālu "to bring": *[lu]-bi-la-ku-um-ma* III 19, *ub-lam-ma* I 28,

abarša "truly": *a-bar-šá* II 69,

abru "wing": *ab-ri-šú* II 85, 120,

abu "father": *a-bi* II 47, 100, AD-*šú* II 46, 99,

agû "crown, tiara": AGA III 109,

ahāmiš "each other": *a-ha-meš* III 140, *a-ha-meš]* II 6,

ahāzu "to grasp, learn": *i-hu-uz-zu* II 158, *i-hu-zu]* I 160, II 159, *i-[hu-z]u* III 166, *[i-hu-zu* I 159, III 164,

ai "may not": *a-a* II 71,

akālu "to eat": *a-kal* II 44, *a-ka-li* II 39, *e-ta-kal* II 52, 67, *ik-kal* II 27, 29, 31, 33, 95, *ik-ka-al* II 80, *ik-ka-la* II 79, 93, 102, *ik-ka-lu* II 27, 29, 31, 33, *i-ku-lu]* II 34, *lu-ku-lu* II 41, *ni-ku-la* II 97, *ta-kal* II 47, *ta-kal]* II 13, *ta-kul* II 135, *ta-ku[l]* II 131,

alādu "to give birth": *a-la-di* II 141, 142, III 12, 13, 15, 75, *a-la-di]* III 22, *a-la-d]i* II 148, *a]-la-di* III 19,

alāku "to go; (vent.) to come": *al-ka* II 14, III 23, 116, *[al]-ka* II 8, *al-k]a-ma* III 70, *[al]-ka-nim-ma* II 97, *a-lik* I 160, II 75, 133, 145, 159, III 165, *i[l-la-ka* II 61, *il-lik* II 89, 150, *[i]l-lik-ma* III 20, *il-[li-kam-ma]* II 54, *it-ta-na-al-lak* II 82, *[it]-ta-na-al-lak* II 109, *lu-[ul-lik* III 18, *lu-ut-[t]al-lak* III 43, *tal-li-ka* III 10,

ālu "city, town": URU I 1, 19, 156, II 155, III 161, URU-*ia* III 43, URU-*šu* III 73, URU.KI U 1,

amāru "to see, behold": *a-mur* II 146, III 106, *e-mur* III 143, *i-mur-ma* II 151,

amatu "word, matter": *a-ma-tum* II 101, *a]-ma-tum* II 99, INIM II 46, 154, [INIM III 1,

amēlu "man": *a-me-la* II 133, *a-me-li]* III 3, *a-me-lu* I 155, II 1, *a-me-lu]* III 4,

ana "to": *ana* I 58, 63, II 72, 86, 96, 154, III 1, 9, 23, 74, 78, 79, 100, 114, *ana]* I 12, III 11, *a-na* II 7, 39, 46, 61, 63, 83, 84, 88, 90, 110, 111, 114, 116, 118, 129, 144, 149, III 36, 42, 43, 50, 116, 125, 129, 131, 135, 137, 138, *a-n[a* II 74, 81, *a-[na* II 40, *[a-na* I 163, II 10, 162, III 169, *[a-na]* I 12, *[a-n]a* II 128, *[a]-na* II 99,

anāku "I": *ana-ku* II 41, *a-na-ku* II 119, III 5, 6, 105, 112, *a-na-ku]* III 113, *a-na-k[u* II 63, *a-n[a-ku* II 9, *[a-n]a-ku* III 103,

annû "this": *an-né-e* II 97, 100,

anzillu "abomination, taboo": *an-zil-la* II 131, *an-z[il-la]* II 13,

apālu "to answer": *ap-pal* II 117, *e-ta-nap-pal-[k]a* III 71,

apātu "numerous": *a-pa-a-ti]* I 13,

appu "nose, top": *ap-pi* II 44, *ap-pi-šá* II 5,

aptu "window": *ap-ti* III 106, 143,

apû "to become (Š: to make) manifest": *šu-pa-a* III 115,

arādu "to descend": *ni-rid-ma* II 97, *tur-rad* II 100, *ur-rad* II 44, *[ur-ra-da-ma* II 79, *ú-ri-dam-ma* II 52, 67, 104, *ú-ri-dam-ma]* I 27, *ú-[ri]-da-ma* II 93,

ardatu "virgin": [KI.SIKIL] III 108,

arkāniš "afterwards": *ár-ka-niš]* III 21,

arki "after, behind": *ár-[k]i-šú* II 106, 108,

armu "mountain goat": *ar-mi* II 28,

arû "eagle": Á.MUŠEN II 5, 7, 10, 26, 29, 30, 35, 36, 37, 40, 46, 63, 94, 96, 101, 105, 114, 116, 127, 129, 147, 154, III 1, 9, 11, 21, 45, 47, 49, 52, 100, 114, 125, 131, 135, 140, Á.MUŠEN] II 71, 152, [Á].MUŠEN III 51, [Á.MUŠEN II 33, 34, 99, 123, III 74, 79, [Á.MU]ŠEN II 80, III 142,

asakku "taboo, forbidden thing": *[a-sak-ka* II 13, *a-sak-ku* II 131,

aslu "ram, sheep": *as-li-ia* II 136, 139,

aṣû "to go out, emerge": È III 91, *a-ṣa-at* II 4, *a-ṣu-ú* III 16, *it-t]a-ṣi* III 84, *li-ṣa-am-ma* II 140, *ú-ṣ[i* II 71,

ašābu "to sit, dwell": *áš-bat* III 108, *uš-[šab]* II 43, *[uš-b]u* I 10,

ašāru "to check, to review": *ú-ši-ir-ma* II 57,

atru "surpassing, superior": *a-tar* II 45, 98,

atmu "hatchling, young of bird or snake": *at-mi* II 39, *at-mu* II 45, *[at]-mu* II 98, *at-mu-ú-a* II 66, *at-mu-ú-šú]* II 66,

atmû "speech, utterance": *at-mi* III 8, *[at-m]i* III 3,

atta "you": *at-ta* II 84, III 10, *at-ta]* II 9, *at-[ta]* III 103, 105,

baʾāru "to catch, hunt": *i-bar-ram-m[a]* II 30, *i-bar-ram-[ma]* II 28, 32, *i-bar-ra[m-ma]* II 26, *i-bar-ru-nik-k[a]* II 48, *i-ba-á[r-ka]* II 47, *l[i-ba-ru-šu]* II 22,

bâʾu "to pass": *i-ba-ʾu-[ú]* III 139, *ni-ba-ʾu-ú* III 104, *n]i-ba-ʾu-ú* III 102,

bābu "gate, doorway": KÁ II 55, III 102, 104, 139, 141, [KÁ.MEŠ] I 17, 18,

bakû "to weep": *i-bak-ki* II 60, *i-ba[k-ki* U 1,

balāṭu "to live": *bul-liṭ-an-ni-ma* II 127,

banû "to build, create": *ba-na-a* I 16, *[ba-nu]-ú* I 11,

baqānu "to pluck": *bu-qu-un-šu-ma* II 86, *[ib-q]u-un-šu-ma* II 121,

barû "to examine, (Gt) to look at thoroughly; (Š) to make see, to reveal": *ab-re-e-ma]* I 162, II 161, *ab-re-e-[m]a* III 168, *bit-ri* II 146, *bit-[r]i* III 127, *ib-ri* II 151, *ú-šab-r]a-a* III 101, *ú-šab-[ra-an-ni* I 59,

bašāmu "to fashion, create": *ba-áš-mu*] I 161, II 160, *b*[*a-áš-m*]*u* III 167,
bašû "to exist": *ib-*[*ši*] III 83, *i-ba-áš-ši* III 22, 39, 132, *i-ba-áš-ši*] III 31, 35, *i-ba-á*[*š*]*-ši* III 126, *i-ba-*[*áš-š*]*i* III 136, [*i-ba-áš-ši* III 24,
bēltu "lady, mistress": GAŠAN III 24, 25,
bēlu "lord": [*be-l*]*í* III 2, *be-lum* II 140, EN-*šú* II 154, III 1,
bēru "double hour; league": KASKAL.GÍD III 30, 38, 44, 46, 48, 124, 130, 134, KASK[AL.GÍD III 34,
bētu "house": É I 64, III 106, [É III 143, É-*su* III 73,
biltu "load": *bi-lat-su* II 54, III 123,
bubūtu "hunger": *bu-bu-ti* II 87, *bu-bu-t*[*i* II 122,
buginnu "trough": *bu-gi-in-ni* III 37,
būlu "cattle": MÁ[Š.ANŠE] II 25, [MÁ]Š.ANŠ[E II 32,
dadmī "habitations": *da-ád-me* I 18,
dagālu "to look": *du-gul* III 126, 132, 136,
daltu "door": GIŠ.IG-[*s*]*a* III 107, [GIŠ.IG-*sa*] III 144,
damāmiš "into (a place of) lamentation": [*da-ma-míš* II 64,
dāmu "blood": *da-am* II 136,
danānu "to be strong, (D) to strengthen": *ú-dan-nin-ma* III 123,
darû "everlasting": *da-ru-ú-ti* II 128,
didānu "bison": *di-da-ni* II 30,
dimtu "tear": *di-ma-a-šú*] II 61,
dintu "tower": [*di*]*-in-ta* II 2,
edēlu "to bar, close": *ú-di-lu* I 17, 18,
edēnû "alone": [*e-d*]*in-nu-ia-a-ma* III 18,
ekallu "palace": É.GAL II 156, [É.GAL I 157, III 162, É.GAL-*ia* I 163, II 162, III 169,
elēnu "above": *e-le-nu* II 59, 117,
elû "to go up; (D) to lift; (adj.) high": *e-li* III 42, *e-li-ma* II 43, *e-li-tu*] II 4, *e-lu-ú* II 24, III 138, *e-*[*te-li* III 20, *ni-li*] II 14, *u*]*l-li-šu-ma* II 38,
emēdu "to lean on, abut": *li-mid-da* III 128,
emû "to become": *i-me*] II 64,
enenna "now": *e-nen-na* II 64,
enūma "when": [*e-n*]*u-ma* U 7,
epēšu "to do, make": DÙ-*uš-ma* II 129, DÙ-[*uš-ma* III 100, *e-piš* II 72, *i-pu-šam-ma* II 10, 154, III 1, *i-pu-šam-m*[*a* II 7, *i-pu-ša*[*m-ma* III 11, *i-pu-š*[*am-ma* III 9, *i-pu-šá-am-ma* II 74, 96, 114, 116, *i-pu-šá-an-ni* II 68, *i-pu-uš-ma* II 40, 144, *i-te-pu-uš* II 2, *ni-pu-uš*] II 8,
erēbu "to enter": *e-re-bi-šu* II 84, *e-re-bi-šú* II 111, [*i-tar-ba-šu*] III 144, *e-tar-ba-áš-*[*šu*] III 107, TU-*ub* II 113,
erēšu "to request": *e-re-ši* II 115,
erṣetu "earth, ground": *er-ṣe-*[*tum* II 69, KI-*t*[*im* II 15, 23, KI-*tum* II 136,
eṣēru "to draw": *i-ṣi-ru* I 3, 156, III 161, *i-ṣi-r*[*u* I 1, II 155,
ešēru "to be, go straight": [*li-še-er*] II 21,
etēqu "to pass through, move on": *e-ti-iq* II 145, *e-ti-i*[*q* II 75, *it-ti-qu* II 49, [*it-ti-qu*] II 17, 19, *i-ti-iq* II 89, 150,
eṭemmu "ghost": *e-ṭém-mu-šu* I 63, *e-ṭém-me* II 137,
ezēbu "to leave, disregard": *e-zi-ib-ma* III 15,
gamāru "to come to an end, finish": *ig-dam-ra* II 138, *ig-dam-ru* II 139,
gišparru "trap": *giš-par-ru* II 22, 48, *giš-par-ru-ka* II 70,
habābu "to murmur": *i-ha-am-b*[*u-ub* III 32,
hadû "to be glad": *li-ih-di* III 78,
hakāmu "to understand": *ih-ta-kim*] III 8, *li-ih-kim-ma*] III 6, *lu-uh-kim*] III 5,
hasīsu "ear, understanding": *ha-si-sa* II 45, 98,
haṭṭu "sceptre": GIŠ.PA I 15,
hâṭu "to check, investigate": *i-ha-aṭ* I 24, *lu-hi-ṭa*] III 18,
iāši "me": *ia-a-ši* I 59, [*i*]*a-a-ši* II 127,
ibru "comrade": *ib-ri* III 12, 23, 31, 35, 39, 42, 115, 126, 132, 136, *ib-*[*ri* III 101, *ib-ri-šú*] II 72,
idu "arm; side": Á-*ia* III 26, Á-*ka*] III 26, Á-*šu* III 28, Á-*šu*] III 28, *i-da-te-šá* III 127, *i-di-ia* III 119, [*i-di-ka*] III 119, *i-di-šu* III 122, *i-d*[*i-šu*] III 122,
idû "to know": *i-*[*d*]*a-a-ma* II 94, *i-di* II 126, *i-du-ú-ma* II 81, *ti-di*] II 68,
ijû "mine": *ia-ú* II 65,
iku "ditch, small canal": *i-ki* III 137,
ilu "god": DINGIR III 101, DINGIR.MEŠ I 2, 4, 29, II 13, 131, 137, 139, DINGIR-*šu* II 3,
ilūtu "divinity": DINGIR-*u-*[*tú* III 110,
ina "in": *ina* I 26, 64, 160, II 4, 5, 16, 18, 50, 53, 55, 84, 100, 104, 111, 112, 123, 139, 140, 152, 159, III 7, 16, 25, 26, 27, 28, 29, 45, 47, 49, 51, 108, 111, 117, 118, 119, 120, 121, 122, 139, 141, 165, [*ina* I 162, II 5, 78, 161, III 22, 168, *i-na* I 14, II 43, 44, 71, 84, 92, 147, U 2, *i-na*] II 121, [*i-na* I 27, II 73, [*i*]*-na* II 125,
inbu "fruit": *in-ba* II 44,
īnu "eye": IGI.2 I 159, II 158, III 164, *i-na-a-a* III 41,
irtu "breast": GABA-*ia* III 117, [GABA-*ka*] III 117, [GABA-*su*] III 120, GABA-*šu* III 120,
isimmānu "food ration, allowance": Z[ÍD.MUNU$_4$] II 63,
isinnu "festival": [EZEN I 12,
iṣṣūru "bird": *iṣ-ṣu-rat* II 79, 93, [*iṣ-ṣ*]*u-ra-a-tu* II 102, [*iṣ-ṣu-r*]*a-ku-ma* III 4, *iṣ-ṣu-ri* II 95, III 3, 8, [MUŠ]EN III 16,
iṣu "tree, wood": *iṣ-ṣi-ma* II 44,
išdu "foundation, base": *iš-di-šá* II 5,
ištēn "one": *iš-tin* III 44, *iš-t*[*in*] III 30, 1-*en* III 124,
išteniš "also, in addition": 1-*niš* I 16,
ištēt "one": 1-*et* III 108,
ištu "after, as soon as": *iš-tu* II 23, 36, III 138,
itbāru "friend": *it-ba-ru* II 9,
itinnu "master builder": *i-tin-ši-na* I 7,
itti "with": *it-ti-ši-n*[*a* II 80, *it-ti* II 95, 101, III 24, *it-t*]*i* III 140, [*it-ti* III 142,
itû "boundary": *i-ta-a* II 17, 19, 49,
kabattu "mind, mood": *kab-t*[*a-as-su* II 12, *kab-ta-ti* II 130,
kabātu "to be weighty; (D) to honour": *ú-kab-bit* II 137,
kakku "weapon": GIŠ.TUKUL II 21,
kalu "all": DÙ III 109, DÙ-*šú-nu* I 12,
kanānu "to coil ": *ka-nin* II 5,
kânu "to be firm, true; (D) to establish": *ú-kin*] I 163, II 162, *ú-*[*ki*]*n* III 169, *ú-kin-nu* I 5,
kapādu "to plan": *ik-pu-du-m*[*a*] II 37, *ik-pu-ud-ma* II 38,
kappu "wing": *kap-pi-ia* III 118, *kap-pi-i*[*a* III

27, *kap-pi-ka*] III 27, [*kap-pi-ka*] III 118, *kap-pi-šu* II 85, III 29, 45, 47, 121, *kap-pi-šu*] III 49, 51, *k*[*ap-pi-šu*] III 121, *kap-pi-šú* II 84, 112, 120, *kap-pi-šú*] III 29,

karšu "stomach; mind": *kar-ši-šú* II 92, *kar-ši-šú*] II 78, *ka-ra-as-su* II 91, [*ka-ra-as-su* II 77,

kasû "to bind": *uk-ta-as-si-ka* II 76,

kaṣāru "to bind, organize": *ka-aṣ-rat* I 14,

kašādu "to reach": *ik-šud-ma* III 73, *ik-šu-dam-ma* III 85, *ik-šu-ud-ma* II 90,

kâša "you": *ka-šá* III 78,

kâši "you": *ka-a-ši* I 61,

kî "as, like; that; how?": [*ki*] II 81, *ki-i* II 117, 126, III 3, 35, 39, 126, 132, 136, *ki-*[*i* III 31, *ki-i-mi* II 102,

kibrāti "regions": *kib-ra-a-ti* I 11, 16,

kibsu "track, trail, path": *kib-su* III 43,

kīma "as, like": GIM I 60, 61, II 115,

KI.MIN (reading uncert.) "ditto, likewise": KI.MIN III 141, KI.MIN] III 142,

kiššatu "world, universe": ŠÚ I 157, II 156, III 162,

kubru "thickness": *ku-bur* II 135,

kubšu "cap, mitre": *ku-ub-šu* I 14,

kullu "to hold": *mu-kil* II 72,

kullumu "to show": *kul-li-man-ni-ma* II 142, *kul-li-man-n*[*i-ma* III 13, *ú-kal-lam-ka* II 148,

kunukku "seal": NA_4.KIŠIB III 106, 143,

kussû "throne, seat": GIŠ.GU.ZA III 110, 111,

kutummu "cover": *ku-tùm* II 110, *ku-tu-um* II 83,

lā "not": *la* I 16, 64, 160, II 47, 81, 86, 132, 159, III 165, *l*[*a*] I 13, [*la* I 14, 15, [*la*] II 100,

labbu "lion": *la-be* III 112, *la-b*[*e*] III 111,

laššu "is not": *la-áš-šu* II 56, 65, III 143, *l*[*a-áš-šu*] III 106,

lemēnu "to be bad, evil": *lem-né-ta-ma* II 130, *le*[*m-né-t*]*a-ma* II 12,

lemniš "badly": *lem-niš* II 18, 50,

lemuttu "evil, misfortune": HUL-*tim* II 72, [HUL-*tim* II 72, *le-mut-tu* II 37, 38,

leqû "to take": *le-qé-a-am* III 17,

lētu "cheek; side, presence": *le-et* III 25,

libbu "heart": *li-ib-bi-šu* U 2, ŠÀ-*ba-šu* II 37, 38, 77, ŠÀ-*ba-šú* II 91, ŠÀ-[*ba-šú* II 42, ŠÀ-*bi* II 83, 84, 100, 110, III 108, š[À-*b*]*i* II 111, ŠÀ-*bi-šá* II 147, ŠÀ-[*bi-šá* II 152, ŠÀ-*bi-šú* II 101,

libittu "brick": *lib-na-a*[*s-su* I 5,

lidānu "young bird, brood of snake": [*li-da-ni-ia*] II 67,

līlāti "evening": *li-la-a-ti* II 53,

lū "let, may, be it": *lu* II 68, *lu-u* I 6, 7, II 9,

lumnu "bad luck, ill fate": *lum-nu* II 68, *lu-mu-un-šú* II 94,

mahāru "to implore, (Gt) to be level, to meet one another, collide": *im-da-har-šu* III 45, 47, *im-da-har-*[*šu* III 49, *im-d*[*a-har-šu* III 51, *im-da-na-ha-ra* II 124, *im-ta-ah-ha-ra* II 134,

mahāṣu "to strike": *ma-hi-ṣi* II 18, [*ma-hi-ṣi* II 50,

mahru "front; before": *mah-ri-ia* I 160, II 159, III 165, *ma-har* II 16,

mahrû "previous, first": I.KÁM I 156,

mala "everything that": *ma-la* I 161, II 160, III 33, 37, 167,

malāku "to advise; (Gt) to take counsel": *im-tal-li-ku* I 10,

malû "to be full; (D) to fill": [*li-mal-li*] II 18, *ú-mal-la*] II 50,

māmītu "oath": *ma-mit* II 16, 22, 23, 48,

mamma "anyone": *mám-ma* I 160, III 165, *mám-*[*ma* II 159,

mannu "who?": *man-nu* II 126,

maqātu "to fall, happen": *im-qut-am-ma*] III 7, *im-qu-ut-ma* III 45, 47, 49, 51,

marāṣu "to become ill, sad; (Š) to make ill, hurt": *i-mar-ra-aṣ*] II 42, *tu-šam-ra-aṣ*] II 12, *tu-šam-ri-iṣ* II 130,

marhītu "wife": [*mar*]-*hi-is-su* I 58,

māru "son; young": DUMU.MEŠ II 34, 36, 41, 95, DUMU.M[EŠ] II 35, DUMU.[MEŠ II 52, DUMU.MEŠ-*šú* II 33, 96, 103, DUMU.MEŠ-*šú*] II 40, DUMU.MEŠ-[*šú*] II 27, 29, 31, DU]MU.M[EŠ-*šú*] II 51,

maṣû "to match, reach; (Št) to penetrate as far as": *uš-ta-ma-aṣ-ṣa* II 110, *uš-ta-ma-a*[*ṣ-ṣ*]*a* II 83,

maššakku "incense": *maš-šak-ki-ia* II 138,

mātu "land, country": KUR.[MEŠ I 29, *ma-a-ti* I 26, III 32, *ma-a-ti*] I 10, *ma-a-tu* III 36, 39, 40, 126, 136, *ma-a-tum* III 35, 132, 133, *ma-a-t*[*um*] III 31, *ma-a-tum-me-e* III 128, *ma-t*]*um* III 88,

mâtu "to die": *a-ma-ta-ma* II 125, *i-ma-*[*ta*] II 122, *li-mu-ta* II 87, *ta-ma-ta-a-ma* II 132,

mênu "crown, tiara": *me-a-nu*] I 14,

milku "advice, counsel": *mi-lik-šú-nu* I 10,

mimmû "everything, every kind of": *mim-mu-ú* II 93, [*mim-mu-ú*] II 79, [*mim*]-*mu-ú* III 5, [*mi*]*m-mu-ú* III 6,

minde "perhaps": *mìn-de* II 100,

mīnu "what? how? why?": [*mi*]-*na-a* III 10, *mì-ni-i* III 31, *mì-n*[*i-i*] III 39, [*mì-ni-i* III 35,

mû "water": *me-e* III 88, 129, 133, *me-e-ma* III 88, 129, *me-*[*e*]-*ma* III 133,

muhhu "top; on, upon": *muh-hi-ia* II 118, UGU I 13, 17, 18, 66, II 104, III 26, 27, 28, 29, 117, 118, 119, 120, 121, 122, UGU-*šu* II 21,

murtappidu "wandering, roving": *mur-tap-pi-du* II 21,

musarû "garden plot": *mu-sa-re-e* III 36,

muššuru "to let go": *ú-maš-šar-ka-ma* II 117,

mutu "husband": *mu-ti* I 60, *mu-ut* I 66,

mūtu "death": *mu-ut* II 87, [*mu-ut*] II 122,

na'ālu "to moisten": *i-n*[*a*]-'*i-il-ma* II 60,

nabalkutu "to turn upside down; befall": *ib-bal-ki-tu-ka-ma* II 48, *li-bal-ki-tu-šu-ma* II 22,

nadānu "to give": *id-nam-ma* II 141, III 12, *lud-din-ka* II 115,

nadû "to throw, cast": *i-di-šú* II 86, *id-di* II 78, 92, *id-*[*di-šu* II 121, *id-du-ú* I 4, *id*]-*du-ú* I 2, *it-ta-di*] II 55, *na-di* II 147, 152, [*na-di-m*]*a* II 123, ŠUB-*ma* III 110,

nagaltû "to wake up": *ag-gal-tam-ma* III 113,

nakāsu "to cut": *nu-uk-kis* II 85, *ú-nak-ki-is* II 120,

nammaštu "wild animal": *nam-maš*]-*ti* II 32,

namru "bright": *na-mir-tum* I 159, II 158, III 164,

nasāhu "to pull out, uproot": *ú-suh-ma* II 143, [*ú-suh-ma* III 14,

nasāku "to throw down, toss": *is-su-ka-áš-šum-ma* III 44, 46, *is-s*[*u-ka-áš-šum-m*]*a* III 48, [*is-su-ka-áš-šum-ma*] III 50,

naṣāru "to watch, guard": *i-na-ṣa-ru* II 25, *i-na-*

ṣ[a-ru II 6,
nāṣu "plumage": *na-aṣ* III 27, 29, 118, 121,
našû "to lift, carry, take": *i-n]a-ši* II 54, *[lu-uš-ši-ka* III 23, *lu-uš-ši-ka-ma* III 116, *[lu-uš-ši-ka-ma]* III 25,
naṭālu "to look, see": *a-na-ṭal* III 40,
nēmequ "wisdom": *[né-me-eq* I 161, II 160, III 167,
nērebu "pass, entrance": *né-reb* III 102, 104, *né-re-[bé-ti* II 20,
nesû "to go far, withdraw": *li-is-su-šu-ma* II 20,
nêʾu "to turn back; to eat, revel": *i-né-eʾ-ú* II 27, 29, 31, *i]-né-eʾ-ú* II 33,
nikkassu "half-reed (a measure of length)": *[n]ik-kàs* III 50,
nīnu "we": *ni-nu* II 97, *ni-nu-u-ma* II 8,
nisqu "choice": *ni-siq* I 159, *ni-siq]* III 164, *[ni-siq* II 158,
nišū "people": UN.MEŠ I 13, UN.[MEŠ I 12,
nuballu "wing": *nu-bal-li-šú* II 120, *n[u-bal-l]i-šú* II 85,
nudunnû "marriage gift, dowry": *nu-dun-na-a* II 115,
nukaribbu "gardener": LÚ.NU.GIŠ.[SAR] III 137,
nurbu "tender part": *nu-ru-ub* II 82,
palāhu "to fear, respect, revere": *ap-làh* II 137,
palāsu "(N) to behold, look at": *ap-pal-sa-am-ma* III 40, *[ip-pal]-sa-ma* II 56, *nap-li-is* III 31, 35, 39,
pānu "face, presence": *pa-an* II 61, *pa-ni-šú* II 106, 108, III 86, *p[a-n]i-šú* II 39,
paqādu "to entrust; to check": *ip-ta-qid* II 105, 107,
parādu "to become scared, frightened": *ap-ta-ru-u[d* III 113,
parakku "dais, sanctuary": *pa-rak-ki* I 24, II 4, *[p]a-rak-ki* II 3, *[pa-rak-ki]* I 16,
pašāru "to solve, explain": *i-pa-šar* III 87,
petû "to open": *ip-te-e-ma* II 91, *[pe]-te-e-ma* II 77,
pīltu "shame": *pil-ta* III 14, *pil-ti* II 143,
pû "mouth, utterance, command": KA-*šá* III 78, KA-*šu* II 7, 10, 40, 74, 116, 144, 154, K[A-*šu*] II 114, KA-*šú* II 129, *pa-a-šu* II 96, *pi-i* III 7, *pi-i-ka* II 140, *pi-i-šu* III 1, 9, 11, *pi-[i]-šu* III 100,
qabû "to say, tell": *a-qab-bu-[ú* III 6, *i-qab-bi* II 101, *i-qab-b[u-ú* III 5, *[qí-bi]-a-am* III 10, *š]u-taq-ba-[at]* III 110,
qaqqaru "ground": *qaq-qa-ra* II 58, *qaq-qa-ri* II 32, III 50,
qatāru "to smoke": *i-qat-tur]* II 59,
qātu "hand": *qa-at* II 18, 50, ŠU-*ka* II 133,
qerbītu "centre, interior": *qer-bit* II 53,
qerbu "inside": *qé-reb* I 163, II 162, *qé-r]eb* III 169, *qé-reb-šá* II 146, 151,
qinnu "nest, family": *qin-na-šú* II 56, *qin-[na-šú* II 65, *qin-ni* II 64, 65, *qin-ni-š[u* II 55,
qurādu "warrior, hero": *qu-ra-di* II 16, 88, 149, *qu-r[a-di* III 7, *[qu-ra-du]* II 62,
rabāṣu "to lie down": *rab-[ṣu]* III 111, *ra-bi-iṣ* II 5, 100,
rabû "to grow; (adj.) great": [GAL.MEŠ] I 2, 4, *[r]a-bu-tum* I 9, *ir-bu-u* II 35, *ir-bu-ú* II 36,
rakāsu "to bind, attach": *ir-ta-kas* III 123,
rapšu "wide, extensive": DAGAL-*tim]* II 15, 23, DAGAL-*tu* III 37, DAGAL-*tum* III 33, 41, DAGAL-*tum]* II 69, *ra-pa-áš-tum* I 158, *ra-pa-áš-tum]* III 163, *ra-p[a-áš-tum* II 157,
rēʾû "shepherd": *re-é-a* I 20, *re-é-[a* I 22, *re-é-um-ši-n[a* I 6,
rêmu "to have pity, mercy on": ARHUŠ-*an-ni-ma* II 115,
rīmu "wild bull": AM II 97, 100, GUD.AM II 26, *ri-me* II 104, *[ri]-mi* II 90, *ri-[mu]* II 76,
rūqu "distant": *[ru-qu-tu]* II 70,
ruṣṣunu "beautiful": *ru-uṣ-ṣu-na-at* III 109,
ruʾu "companion, friend": *ru-u$_8$-a-šú* II 39,
ruʾūtu "friendship": *ru-u$_8$-a-u-tu* II 11, *ru-u$_8$-a-[u-tu* II 8,
sadāti (mng. uncert.): *sa-da-a-ti* II 82, 109,
sahāru "to turn around; (Št) to surround, encircle": *i-sah-hu-ra* II 118, *šu-tas-hu-ru* I 19,
sakāpu "to push back, overthrow": *a-sa-kip-ma* III 107, *i-sa-kip-ma* III 144,
sanāqu "to check, examine; to come close": *as-niq* I 162, II 161, *as-niq]* III 168, *a-sa-an-ni-qa-ak-ka* II 132,
santakku "cuneiform wedge": *sa-an-tak-ki* I 161, II 160, *sa-an-tak-k]i* III 167,
sapāhu "to scatter": *sa-ap-hu* II 66,
sappāru "mountain ram": *sa-ap-pa-ri* II 30,
serremu "onager": *sír-ri-mu* II 26,
ṣabātu "to seize": *iṣ-ṣa-bat-su* II 112, *li-iṣ-bat* II 133, *ṣa-bat-su* II 84,
ṣabītu "gazelle": MAŠ.DÁ.MEŠ II 28,
ṣâdu "to prowl, roam about": *iṣ-ṣu-da* III 21,
ṣapāru "to press down, inlay, inset": *ṣa-ap-rat]* I 15,
ṣarbutu "poplar": *ṣa[r-ba-tu* II 4,
ṣehru "small; child": *ṣe-eh-ru* II 45, 98,
ṣerru "snake": MUŠ II 7, 27, 28, 31, 32, 54, 60, 73, 74, 89, 90, 100, 112, 114, 116, MUŠ] II 5, 52, [MUŠ] II 10, MUŠ-*mi* II 41, 42,
ṣēru "open country, plain; back, upperside": EDIN II 32, *ṣe-er* II 90,
ṣillu "shadow": GIŠ.MI II 4,
ṣīru "exalted": *ṣi-(ru)* I 3,
ṣītu "exit": *ṣi-is-su* III 77, *ṣi-t[i-šú* III 16,
ṣubbû "to observe": *ṣu-ub-bi* III 127,
ṣummû "to thirst": *ṣu-mi]-i* II 122,
ṣūmu "thirst": *ṣu-um-mi* II 87,
ṣupru "nail, claw": *[ṣú]-up-ra-nu-uš-šú* II 58,
ša "that; what; of": *ša* II 86, 157, 159, III 22, *[ša* I 158, 160, III 163, 165, *šá* II 3, 11, 13, 17, 19, 20, 39, 47, 49, 68, 73, 106, 108, 119, 131, 133, 141, 142, 148, III 3, 12, 13, 15, 19, 32, 53, 75, 102, 104, 137, 138, *[šá* I 10, III 116, *[šá]* II 17,
šāʾiltu "female dream interpreter, pythia": MÍ.EN.ME.LI.MEŠ II 138,
šadû "mountain; desert": KUR-*a* II 145, III 18, 128, KUR-*e* III 22, KUR-*e]* II 20, *šá-da-a* II 24, 89, *šá-da-a]* II 75, 150, III 20, *[šá-da-a* II 14,
šahāṭu "to leap, attack": *i[š-tah-ṭu-(ni)]* III 112,
šakānu "to place, set": *a-šak-ka-nu-ka* II 119, *iš-kun* II 39, *iš-ku[n]* III 86, *iš-ku-nu* I 13, *iš-ta-kan* III 120, 121, 122, *iš-ta-ka[n* III 28, *[iš-ta-kan* III 29, *šak-na-ku* II 126, *šá-ki-[nu* I 11, *šuk-na-an-ni* II 143, III 14, *šu-kun* III 27, 43, 117, 118, 119, *[šu-kun* III 26,
šalāmu "to be sound, safe": *ša[l-mu* II 66, *šá-li-im]* II 65,

šalšu "third": *šal-šá* III 38, 48, 134, 3.KÁM III 161,

šamāmū "heaven": *šá-ma-mi* II 43, *šá-ma-m*[*i* II 59, *šá-ma-mì* II 79, 93,

šamû "heaven": AN-*e* I 24, 27, III 42, 116, 138, AN-*e*] III 23, AN-*ú* II 70,

šammu "drug, plant": *šam-ma* II 141, 142, *šam-m*[*a* II 148, *š*]*am-ma* III 13, [*šam-ma* III 19, [*šam-m*]*a* III 15, [*ša*]*m-ma* III 12, *šam-mu* III 22, 75, *šam-mu*] III 24,

šamšu "sun": ^{d}UTU-*ši* II 86,

šanû "second; to do for a second time": *iš-ni-i'* II 107, *šá-na-a* III 34, 46, 2-*a* III 130, 2.KÁM II 155,

šapla "under": *šap-la* III 111,

šapāru "to send": *a-šap-pa-rak-ka* II 133,

šaqû "to be high; (D) to lift, raise": *ul-taq-qa-áš-šú* II 153, *ú-šá-qí-šu-ma*] III 34, [*ú-šá-qí-šu-ma*] III 30, *ú-šá-qí-šú-ma* III 134, *ú-šá-q*[*í-šú-m*]*a* III 124, *ú-šá-q*[*í*]-*šú-ma* III 130,

šarāku "to present, endow": *áš-ru-uk*] II 63, *iš-ru-ku-uš*] I 158, II 157, *iš-*[*ru-ku-u*]*š* III 163,

šarru "king": LUGAL I 21, 23, 26, 157, II 156, III 162, LUGA]L I 6, [LUGAL I 13, II 156, LUGAL.MEŠ I 160, II 159, III 165, *šar-ru* I 62,

šarrūtu "kingship": LUGAL-*ú-tu* I 27,

šasû "to shout; (Gtn) to read": *ši-ta-si-ia* I 163, II 162, III 169,

šāšu "(to) him, that": *šá-a-šú* II 4, *šá-šu-ma* III 114, 125, 131, 135, *šá-šu-ma*] III 74, 79, *šá-šu-m*[*a* I 58,

šattu "year": MU.AN.NA III 84,

šatû "to drink": *taš-ti-i* II 136,

šaṭāru "to write": *áš-ṭur* I 162, II 161, III 168,

šaṭāṭu "to rip, tear open": [*iš*]-*ṭu-uṭ* II 91, *šu-ṭu-uṭ*] II 77,

še'û "to seek": *iš-te-né-'e-e-ma* I 25, *iš-te-né-e'-i* II 82, 106, 108, *i-še-'i-i* I 21, *i-še-*['*i-i* I 23,

šebû "to be satisfied, get sated with": *i-šeb-ba-a* III 41,

šemû "to hear, heed": *iš-ma-a* II 51, 103, *iš-me-šu-nu-ti-ma* II 51, *iš-me-šú-nu-ti-ma* II 103, *lu-uš-te-eš-me* II 128, *še-mi-šu*] II 73,

šērtu "crime, punishment": *še-er-ta* II 119, *še-ret-ka* II 118, 126,

šētu "web": *še-et-ka* II 69, *še-e-tu* II 47, *še-ti-ka* II 71,

šiāhu "to grow tall": *i-ši-hu* II 35, 36,

šiāmu "to decree, destine": *i-ši-mu*] I 12, *mu-šim-mu* I 9,

šibirru "staff": *ši-bir-r*[*u* I 8,

šikittu "creation": *ši-kit-ti*] I 11,

šīmtu "fate, destiny": *ši-ma-te*] I 9,

šipru "art, skill": *šip-ru* I 160, II 159, III 165,

šīru "flesh": *ši-i-ra* II 93, 95, *š*[*i-ra*] II 102, UZU II 55, 82, 97, 105, 107, UZU] II 79, 80, U[ZU II 54,

šû "he, that": *š*]*u-u* II 11, *šu-u-ma* III 101, *šu-ú* III 5, 6, [*šu-ú* III 4,

šuātu "that": *šu-a-tu* I 160, II 159, *šu-a-t*]*u* III 165,

šu'u "sheep": *šu-'e-e-a* II 135,

šubtu "seat, ambush": *šu-ub-ta* II 78, 92,

šukênu "to prostrate oneself": *nu-uš-ke-nu* III 103, [*nu-uš-ke-nu*] III 105, *uš-*[*ke-nu*] III 140,

šuklulu "to perfect": *ul-tak-li-lu-šú*] I 1, 156, II 155, *ul-tak-li-lu*]-*šú* III 161, *ul-*[*tak-li-lu-šú*] I 3,

šumu "name": MU-*šú* I 155, II 1, *šu-ma* II 143, *š*]*u-ma* III 14,

šuttatu "pit": *šu-ut-ta-ti* II 86, 125, *šu-ut-ta*]-*ti* II 123, *šu-ut-*[*ta-ti*] II 121, *šu-ut-ta-tum* II 146, 151,

šuttu "dream": MÁ[Š.MI-*ka*] III 115, [*šu-ut-ta*] III 101, [*šu-u*]*t-tu* I 59,

tabāku "to pour, shed": *ú-tab-bi-ku-šú* III 72,

takālu "to trust": *at-kal-kúm-ma* II 62,

tāmartu "observation, viewing": *ta-mar-ti* I 163, II 162, III 169,

tāmtu "sea": *tam-tum* III 33, 37, 41, 127, 129, 137,

tamû "to swear": *it-mu-ú* II 23, *it-*[*mu-ú*] II 16, *ni-it-ma-a* II 15,

tarāku "to throb, pound": *i-tar-rak* III 52,

tarbāṣu "courtyard, pen": *tar-ba-ṣi* III 33,

târu "to return; to turn into": *it-tur* III 36, [*i-tur* III 21, *i-tu-ra* III 129, 137,

tebû "to rise, get up": *at-be-ma* III 112,

tēqītu "oinment, daubing": *te-qí-tu* III 76,

tikpu "spot, mark": *ti-kip* I 161, II 160, III 167,

turbu'tu "dust (storm)": *tur-bu-u'-ta-šú* II 59,

ṭabāhu "to slaughter": *ṭu-ub-bu-hi* II 139,

ṭuppu "tablet": DUB II 155, [DUB I 156, III 161, *ṭup-pa-a-ni* I 162, II 161, III 168,

ṭupšarrūtu "scribal art": *ṭup-šar-ru-ti*] I 159, II 158, *ṭup-š*[*ar-ru-t*]*i* III 164,

u "and": *u* II 9, III 73, 103, 104, 105, 139, 141, *u*] III 102, *ù* I 15, 21, 23, 64, II 85, 87, 106, 108, 122, III 33, 37, 41,

ukultu "food": *ú-kul-ta* II 34,

ul "not": *ul* II 51, 57, 95, 103, III 22, 41, 42, 83, *u*[*l*] III 40, [*ul* III 3, [*u*]*l* II 103,

ullānumma "thereupon, immediately": *ul-la-nu-um-ma* II 153,

ūmišam "daily": UD-*mi-šam-ma* II 6, UD-*mì-šam-ma* II 124, 134, UD.1.KÁM.TA.ÀM II 25,

ummānu "troops; crowd, common people": *um-ma-ni* I 17,

ūmu "day": UD-*me* II 53, UD-*mi* II 128, UD-*mi-šu-ma* I 14,

unnēnu "supplication": *un-né-ni* II 73,

uqnû "lapis lazuli": NA_4.ZA.GÌN I 15,

urhu "road": *ur-ha* II 75, 145, *u*[*r-ha* II 150,

uššū "foundation": [*uš-ši-šú* I 2, [*uš-š*]*i-šú* I 4,

uznu "ear, understanding": *uz-nu* I 158, II 157, III 163,

uzuzzu "to stand, to be present": *it-ta-ziz* II 104,

zakāru "to pronounce, call": *iz-z*[*ak*]-*kar* III 131, *iz-*[*zak-ka*]*r* III 135, *iz-zak-k*[*ar-š*]*ú* III 125, *i-zak-kar* II 40, 99, *i-zak-kar*] III 1, [*i-zak-kar*] II 154, *i-zak-kar-šu* III 74, *i-*[*zak-kar-šu*] III 79, *i-zak-kar-šú* II 114, 129, 144, III 9, 11, *i-zak-kar-šú*] I 58, II 7, 10, 74, III 100, *i-zak-*[*ka*]*r-šú* II 116, [*i-zak-kar-šú*] III 114, *i-zak-ka-ra* II 96, M[U]-*ár* II 46,

zamāru "to sing": *az-mu-ur* U 3,

zaqāpu "to erect; (Gt) to rise, get up": *iz-zaq-pu-nim-ma* II 24, *ni-zaq-pa-am-ma* II 14,

zikru "name; utterance, command": *z*[*i*]-*ik-ri* I 12, *zi-kir* II 88, 103, 149, [*zi-kir* II 51, *zi-kir-ka* II 128,

zīmu "appearance, countenance": [M]ÚŠ-[*šá*] III 109,

Index of Names

Personal Names

Aššūr-bāni-apli (Assurbanipal, king of Assyria): ᵐAN.ŠÁR—DÙ—DUMU.UŠ I 157, II 156, III 162,

Etāna (king of Kish): ᵈ*e-ta-na* I 62, II 134, 144, 150, III 11, 114, 125, 131, 135, 142, U 5, ᵈ*e-t*]*a-na* III 9, ᵈ*e*-[*ta-na* III 140, ᵈ*e*-[*ta-na*] III 100, [ᵈ*e-ta-na* III 8, [ᵈ*e*]-*ta-na* U 8, ᵈ*e-ta-ni* III 74, 79, *e-t*[*a-na* III 53, [*e-t*]*a-na* I 7, *e-ta-ni* I 58, 60,

Place Names

Kīš (city in Babylonia, now Ingharra/Uhaimir): KIŠ.KI U 1, 4, [KIŠ].KI U 6, [KIŠ.K]I I 3,

Māt Aššūr (Assyria): KUR—AN.ŠÁR.KI] I 157, II 156, KUR—AN.ŠÁR.K]I III 162,

God Names

Adad (weather god): ᵈIM II 3, III 104, 141,

Anu (god of heaven): ᵈ*a-nim* III 102, 139, ᵈ*a-nim*] III 116, ᵈ*a*-[*nim*] III 138,

Anunnakkū (a designation of the infernal gods): ᵈ*a-nun-na-k*[*i* I 9,

Anzû (a mythical eagle): *an-zu-ú* II 72,

Ēa (god of wisdom): ᵈÉ.A III 139, ᵈÉ.[A III 102,

Igīgū (a designation of the great gods): ᵈ5.1.1 I 5, 12, 19,

Illil (Enlil, king of gods): ᵈ⁺EN.LÍL I 24, III 139, ᵈ⁺EN.LÍ[L III 102,

Ištār (Ishtar, goddess of love): ᵈ*in-nin-na* I 22, ᵈIŠ.TAR I 20, III 24, 25, 104, 141,

Nabû (Nebo, divine scribe): ᵈAG I 158, 161, II 157, 160, III 163, 167,

Sebettu ("the Seven Gods"; Pleiades): ᵈ*se-bet-tum* I 17,

Sîn (Moon, god of understanding): ᵈ3[0 III 141, ᵈ30 III 104,

Šamaš (Sun, god of justice): ᵈUTU II 16, 17, 18, 19, 22, 47, 48, 49, 50, 61, 62, 69, 74, 88, 117, 124, 129, 135, 144, 149, 154, III 1, 7, 104, 141, ᵈU[TU II 68, [ᵈUTU II 11, ᵈUTU-*ši* II 134,

Tašmētu (bride of Nabû): ᵈ*taš-me-tum* I 158, II 157, III 163,

broken: ᵈ*x* I 59,

Index of Manuscripts

By Museum Number and/or Excavation Number

Neo-Assyrian

Middle Assyrian

Old Babylonian

Concordance of the Sigla Assigned to the Exemplars

SAA Etana	Haul Etana	Saporetti Etana	Kinnier Wilson Etana
A	A	I	A
-	-	U	B
C	C	W	C
B_1	D	L	D
B_2	Em	J	E
B_3	Ep	M	E
F	F	A, T	F
G	G	B	G
H	H	D	H
-	-	-	I
J	J	N	J
K	K	E	K
L	L	V	L
M	M	F	M
N	N	C, G	N
O	O	H	O
-	-	-	P
OB_M	OV-I	K	OV_1
OB_S	OV-II	P	OV_2
-	-	-	OV_3
MA_1	MA-I	Q	MA_1
MA_2	MA-II	R	MA_2
MA_3	MA-III	S	MA_3
MA_4	MA-IV	O	MA_4
-	-	-	MA_5

Concordance of Tablet and Episode Numbers

SAA Etana	Haul Etana	Saporetti Etana	Kinnier Wilson Etana
Old Babylonian			
	OV-I i	I, 1	I/A
	OV-I ii	I, 3	I/B
	OV-II	II, 1-3	I/C
	OV-I v	II, 4-5	I/D
	OV-I vi	III, 1-2	I/E
			II/A
Middle Assyrian			
	MA-I ii	II, 1-2	I/A
	MA-I iii	II, 4-5	I/B
	MA-IV	II, 6	I/C
	MA-II obv.	III, 1	I/D
	MA-II rev.	III, 1	I/E
	MA-I iv	III, 2	I/F
	MA-I v	III, 2	I/G
	MA-III	III, 5	I/H
			II/A
Neo-Assyrian			
I	I	I, 1	I/A
III 70-92	Fragmente	III, 1, 3	I/B
II	II	I, 2; II, 1-6	II
III 9-19	III obv. 9-19	III, 4-5	III/A
			III/B
Uncertain	Fragmente	III, 7	IV/A
III 100-142	III rev. 1-43	III, 2-3	IV/B
III 1-56	III obv.	III, 4-6	IV/C
III 124-144	III rev. 25-60	III, 3	IV/D
			IV/E
I 57-66	I 1′-10′	III, 1	V/A

Concordance of Tablet and Episode Numbers II

SAA Etana	**Dalley,** ***Myths***	**B.R. Foster,** ***Before the Muses***
Neo-Assyrian		
I	I	I/A
I 57-66	III, between K 14788 and III 100-163 of SAA Etana	
II	II	II
III 1-56	III [obverse]	III/A, IV/C
III 70-91		
III 100-163	III [reverse] after I 57-66 of SAA Etana	III/B
K 14788	III, between III 1-56 and I 57-66 of SAA Etana	

SIGN LIST

No.	Value	Count
001	*aš*	1
	ina	49
005	*ba*	31
006	*ṣú*	1
	zu	8
007	*su*	18
009	*bal*	4
	pal	4
010	*ád*	1
012	*qut*	1
	tar	6
	TAR	5
013	*an*	18
	d	82
	AN	14
	DINGIR	10
015	*ka*	60
	INIM	3
	KA	9
035	*nak*	1
038	URU	8
055	*la*	46
057	*mah*	3
058	*tu*	31
	TU	2
059	*le*	6
	li	41
	LI	1
060e	MUNU$_4$	1
061	*mu*	33
	MU	4
062	*qa*	9
068	*ru*	38
	ŠUB	1
069	*bat*	4
	be	5
	mid	1
	mit	4
	ziz	1
070	*na*	116
	NA	1
072	*kul*	5
073	*ti*	53
074	*bar*	6
	maš	3
	MAŠ	1
075	*nu*	34
	NU	1
076	MÁŠ	3
077	*kun*	8
078	*bak*	2
	hu	11
	MUŠEN	48
079	*nam*	5
080	*eq*	3
	ig	2
	ik	19
	iq	4
	IG	2
081	*mut*	2
083	*rad*	2
	rat	4
084	*zi*	7
085	*gi*	1

No.	Value	Count
086	*re*	11
	ri	37
	tal	3
	ṭal	1
087	*nun*	1
	zil	2
088	*kab*	3
	kap	16
094	*tim*	6
097	*ag*	1
	ak	1
	AG	6
099	*en*	3
	EN	6
102	*suh*	2
	MÚŠ	1
104	*sa*	17
108	*ṭur*	3
112	*se*	1
	si	6
115	*sak*	2
	šak	3
124	*tab*	1
	tap	1
126	*šum*	4
	tak	8
	taq	2
128	*ab*	5
	ap	11
129	*nap*	4
130	*uk*	3
131	*as*	10
	aṣ	9
	az	1
133	KÁ	7
134	*ṭup*	6
	um	6
	DUB	3
139	*ta*	86
	TA	1
142	*i*	150
142a	*ia*	24
143	*kan*	5
	KÁM	4
144	*tur*	5
	DUMU	17
145	*at*	19
	aṭ	1
	AD	2
147	*ṣe*	4
	ṣi	14
148	*in*	4
149	*rab*	1
151	LUGAL	15
152	*šar*	6
	EZEN	1
	SAR	1
166	*kas*	1
	KASKAL	9
167	*qab*	3
	GABA	4
168	EDIN	1
169	*tah*	1
170	*am*	12
	AM	3

No.	Value	Count
171	UZU	8
172	*kúm*	1
	pil	2
	NE	2
183	*ram*	4
191	*qu*	15
192	*kàs*	1
205	*il*	6
206	*du*	9
207	*tum*	32
208	ANŠE	2
211	*uš*	23
	UŠ	3
212	*iš*	28
	IŠ	5
214	*bé*	1
	bi	24
215	*šim*	1
228	*kib*	3
	kip	5
229	NA4	3
230	*qaq*	3
	DÀ	1
	DÙ	7
231	*lí*	1
	né	19
	ni	49
232	*er*	4
	ir	4
233	*mal*	2
237	DAGAL	6

No.	Value	Count
271	ARHUŠ	1
295	*pa*	22
	PA	1
295k	*šab*	3
	šap	2
296	*giš*	3
	is	11
	iṣ	14
	iz	4
	GIŠ	8
297	GUD	1
298	*al*	9
306	*ár*	5
	ub	10
	up	1
307	*mar*	5
308	*e*	75
309	*lud*	1
312	*un*	4
	UN	2
313	*kit*	1
	qid	2
	sah	1
	LÍL	3
314	*lak*	4
	ret	2
	rid	1
	KIŠIB	2
318	*šam*	21
	ú	63
321	*làh*	1
322	*dan*	1
	kal	12

No.	Sign	Value	Count
		reb	7
324		*bet*	1
		bit	4
		é	3
		É	12
328		*ra*	35
330		LÚ	1
332		*zak*	22
		zaq	2
334		*et*	3
		id	7
		it	19
		Á	51
335		*da*	27
		ṭa	1
339		*áš*	28
342		*ma*	188
343		*gal*	1
		GAL	8
346		*kir*	5
		piš	1
		qer	1
347		*mir*	3
		AGA	1
349		*bur*	1
350		GAŠAN	2
353		*ša*	8
354		*qat*	1
		šu	102
		ŠU	1
355		*lib*	1
366		*lat*	2

No.	Sign	Value	Count
		GÌN	1
		KUR	9
367		*še*	10
371		*bu*	15
		pu	18
		sír	1
		GÍD	9
372		*uṣ*	1
		uz	4
373		*šud*	1
374		MUŠ	20
376		*te*	12
377		*kar*	23
379		:	32
381		*par*	3
		tam	7
		tú	1
		ud	4
		ut	16
		uṭ	2
		UD	7
		UTU	29
382		È	1
383		*pe*	1
		pi	25
384		ŠÀ	14
396		*hi*	6
		ŠÁR	6
397		*'e*	2
		'i	3
		'u	3
		e'	7
		i'	1
		u'	1

No.	Value	Count
398	*ah*	1
	eh	2
	ih	3
	uh	1
399	*im*	13
	IM	3
400	*bir*	1
401	*har*	5
	mur	5
406	*kam*	1
411	*u*	18
412	UGU	17
420	*liṭ*	1
425	*kis*	1
	kiš	1
	KIŠ	4
427	*mi*	18
	MI	2
429	*gul*	3
433	*nim*	6
434	*tùm*	1
435	*lam*	2
440	*kim*	3
	ṭém	2
	GIM	3
441	*ul*	21
449	*lem*	4
	ši	39
	IGI	3
451	*ar*	2
455	*ù*	12
456	HUL	2
457	*de*	1
	di	34
461	*ke*	3
	ki	29
	qé	6
	qí	7
	KI	14
465	*din*	2
	tin	3
467	*dun*	1
469	*šuk*	2
471	*man*	3
	mìn	1
	niš	4
472	*eš*	1
	30	2
480	*ana*	21
	1	14
483	*kil*	1
491	*ṣar*	1
494	u_8	3
515	*bul*	1
532	*me*	27
	mì	7
	šeb	1
	šip	3
	ME	1
533	*meš*	2
	míš	1
	MEŠ	34
535	*ib*	18
	ip	4

No.	Value	Count
536	*ku*	29
	KU	2
	TUKUL	1
	ZÍD	1
537	*lu*	33
538	*kin*	4
	qin	5
545	*šú*	77
	ŠÚ	3
554	*mám*	3
	mim	4
	rak	6
	šal	4
	MÍ	1
555	*ṣu*	14
556	*nen*	1
	nin	3
557	*dam*	8
559	GU	2
563	*nik*	2
	niq	3
564	SIKIL	1
565	*lum*	2
570	MIN	2
	2	5
575	*lik*	11
	tas	1
	taš	4
	ur	6
579	*a*	173
	A	2
580	ÀM	1
586	*ṣa*	10
	ZA	3
589	*ha*	11
592	*siq*	3
593	3	1
595	*ṭu*	4
597	*šá*	81
598	5	3

State Archives of Assyria

VOLUME I
THE CORRESPONDENCE OF SARGON II, PART I
Letters from Assyria and the West
Edited by Simo Parpola
1987

VOLUME II
NEO-ASSYRIAN TREATIES AND LOYALTY OATHS
Edited by Simo Parpola and Kazuko Watanabe
1988

VOLUME III
COURT POETRY AND LITERARY MISCELLANEA
Edited by Alasdair Livingstone
1989

VOLUME IV
QUERIES TO THE SUNGOD
Divination and Politics in Sargonid Assyria
Edited by Ivan Starr
1990

VOLUME V
THE CORRESPONDENCE OF SARGON II, PART II
Letters from the Northern and Northeastern Provinces
Edited by Giovanni B. Lanfranchi and Simo Parpola
1990

VOLUME VI
LEGAL TRANSACTIONS OF THE ROYAL COURT OF NINEVEH, PART I
Tiglath-Pileser III through Esarhaddon
Edited by Theodore Kwasman and Simo Parpola
1991

VOLUME VII
IMPERIAL ADMINISTRATIVE RECORDS, PART I
Palace and Temple Administration
Edited by F. M. Fales and J. N. Postgate
1992

VOLUME VIII

ASTROLOGICAL REPORTS TO ASSYRIAN KINGS

Edited by Hermann Hunger

1992

VOLUME IX

ASSYRIAN PROPHECIES

Edited by Simo Parpola

1997

VOLUME X

LETTERS FROM ASSYRIAN AND BABYLONIAN SCHOLARS

Edited by Simo Parpola

1993

VOLUME XI

IMPERIAL ADMINISTRATIVE RECORDS, PART II

Provincial and Military Administration

Edited by F. M. Fales and J. N. Postgate

1995

VOLUME XII

GRANTS, DECREES AND GIFTS OF THE NEO-ASSYRIAN PERIOD

Edited by L. Kataja and R. Whiting

1995

VOLUME XIII

LETTERS FROM PRIESTS TO THE
KINGS ESARHADDON AND ASSURBANIPAL

Edited by Steven W. Cole and Peter Machinist

1998

State Archives of Assyria Studies

VOLUME I
Neuassyrische Glyptik des 8.-7. Jh. v. Chr.
unter besonderer Berücksichtigung der Siegelungen
auf Tafeln und Tonverschlüsse
by Suzanne Herbordt
1992

VOLUME II
The Eponyms of the Assyrian Empire 910–612 BC
by Alan Millard
1994

VOLUME III
The Use of Numbers and Quantifications
in the Assyrian Royal Inscriptions
by Marco De Odorico
1995

VOLUME IV
Nippur in Late Assyrian Times
c. 755–612 BC
by Steven W. Cole
1996

VOLUME V
Neo-Assyrian Judicial Procedures
by Remko Jas
1996

VOLUME VI
Die neuassyrischen Privatrechtsurkunden
als Quelle für Mensch und Umwelt
by Karen Radner
1997

VOLUME VII
References to Prophecy in Neo-Assyrian Sources
by Martti Nissinen
1998

VOLUME VIII

Die Annalen des Jahres 711 v. Chr.
nach Prismenfragmenten aus Ninive und Assur
by Andreas Fuchs
1998

VOLUME IX

The Role of Naqia/Zakutu in Sargonid Politics
by Sarah C. Melville
1999

VOLUME X

Herrschaftswissen in Mesopotamien:
Formen der Kommunikation zwischen Gott und König
im 2. und 1. Jahrtausend v.Chr.
by Beate Pongratz-Leisten
1999

VOLUME XI

The King's Magnates
A Study of the Highest Officials of the Neo-Assyrian Empire
by Raija Mattila
2000

VOLUME XII

A Survey of Neo-Elamite History
by Matthew W. Waters
2000

VOLUME XIII

A Sketch of Neo-Assyrian Grammar
by Jaakko Hämeen-Anttila
2000

State Archives of Assyria Cuneiform Texts

VOLUME I
The Standard Babylonian Epic of Gilgamesh
by Simo Parpola
1997

VOLUME II
The Standard Babylonian Etana Epic
by Jamie R. Novotny
2001

Melammu Symposia

VOLUME I
The Heirs of Assyria
Proceedings of the Opening Symposium of
The Assyrian and Babylonian Intellectual Heritage Project
Held in Tvärminne, Finland, October 8-11, 1998
Edited by Sanna Aro and R.M. Whiting
2000

Other Titles

The Prosopography of the Neo-Assyrian Empire
VOLUME 1: A-G
Edited by Karen Radner
1998/99
VOLUME 2/I: H-K
Edited by Heather Baker
2000

ASSYRIA 1995
Proceedings of the 10th Anniversary Symposium of
The Neo-Assyrian Text Corpus Project
Helsinki, September 7-11, 1995
Edited by S. Parpola and R.M. Whiting
1997

NINEVEH, 612 BC
The Glory and Fall of the Assyrian Empire
Catalogue of the 10th Anniversary Exhibition of
The Neo-Assyrian Text Corpus Project
Edited by Raija Mattila
1995